The *Bugle* *Sounds*

LIFE IN THE
FOREIGN LEGION

A SOLDIER OF THE LEGION

would not have wished to serve France. But that matters little, for in addition to France they are serving civilization. Everywhere the Legion goes roads are made, houses are built. Here the European is fulfilling to the utmost his duty as practical educator. In Morocco one is shown the city, Volubilis, which the Roman Legions built. In a few centuries one will be shown the work of the Foreign Legion inscribed in this rich soil in the shade of palmeries. When one thinks of the leader, Marshall Lyautey, who has made this success possible, old Roman words come to one's lips. One is eager to call him Proconsul and to give him the surname "Africanus."

Three years ago I did not know Morocco. When, along with other French writers, I was asked to go there, I remember that I set out in a skeptical frame of mind. What was I going to find down there? Doubtless two civilizations in juxtaposition to each other and not understanding each other—hostile natives and discontented Frenchmen. It did not take me long to see that my impression was wrong. What I saw was a country where everything had been done well, where the roads were more beautiful than the roads of Europe, the factories more efficient, the hygiene more perfect. Here the cities were built with a thought for art and for order which exists nowhere else to the same extent. Here Arab pashas meted out .justice under the protection of French power. An ancient civilization had been saved without denying it the technical advantages of the West. English business men and American writers traveled with me. All expressed their admiration. I recall no circumstance in which I have received such an impression of success better achieved.

In the building of this success the Foreign Legion has played a great part. It is far more than a military organization; it is an institution. As I have talked with Major Pechkoff, I have come to appreciate the almost religious character of this institution. A man does not join the Foreign Legion the way he joins the average regiment, with the idea of getting out at the end of two or three years and not giving it another thought. A man gives the Legion his life. Far from the Legion, a man is always an officer or soldier of the Legion. Major Pechkoff has told me that he has seen soldiers of the Legion dying in hospitals, insensible to everything which surrounds them. But when officers of the Legion come to their bedsides, they salute.

And when Major Pechkoff, his eyes shining with faith, speaks of his men with that human and direct simplicity which the reader will love in his book, his friends think: "an Apostle."

ANDRÉ MAUROIS.

CONTENTS

CONTENTS

INTRODUCTION

In the forests and hills of Indo-China, in the outposts pitched high on the crests of the mountains of Morocco, in the scattered fortresses of the Algerian desert, the bugle of the Foreign Legion sounds.

The natives of these remote places rejoice when they hear this sound. They feel safe, they feel sure of to-morrow, they know that they can work in peace and security; that they will gather what they sow. . . .

As for the legionnaire himself, his whole life moves to the sound of the bugle. It brings him news of victory or defeat. It calls him to fight and to rest; it tells him to advance, to halt, to open fire or to charge. It wakes him up at dawn; it puts him to sleep at night.

The buglers are chosen from among those of the legionnaires who are most tireless on march, who are bravest in battle. Seldom has a bugler been known to die in bed: he dies in the midst of battle, his bugle at his lips.

Modestly and humbly I offer here the pages of

my diary under the title, *The Bugle Sounds.*
Read with an open heart this fragmentary account
of a few of the exploits of the French Foreign
Legion in Morocco.

The summer of 1925 found me in the Military
Hospital in Rabat, Morocco, recovering from a
wound in my left foot, received while fighting against
the Riffian forces.

I had much leisure to think and to recall the years
of my service in Morocco with the French Foreign
Legion.

It was then I decided that I owed a tribute of
recognition to the men with whom I had been asso-
ciated for many years and from whose ranks I came.
I have tasted the same salt of the sweat that ran
down their faces. I owe homage to these unknown
soldiers of fortune, to these nomadic builders who,
under the torrid heat of Africa, are carrying their
houses on their backs, blowing up rocks to make
roads, calcinating stones in kilns to make lime for
buildings and performing all the constructive work
necessary in a new country.

They have a right to say as the Romans did: "We
are marching and the road follows us." In mountainous regions where there was not even the slight-
est trail they have built good roads. The legionnaires have always been wonderful fighting men,
xii

but between fights they have become carpenters, road-builders, miners and masons. They have made it possible for other men to live in peace and harmony in this far-away country. It is only under the protection of the outposts which they have built that civilization can develop in Morocco.

They are simple and they are modest, the men of the Foreign Legion. They do not claim glory for their services. They do not even claim recognition. But their enthusiasm, the wonderful effort that they make, the great force that they put into everything they do, will not disappear, and cannot remain unnoticed by all those who have seen them at work. The most impressive thing about them is that they do not think of themselves as heroes sacrificing their lives. They do not think of themselves as martyrs; and even if they die, they die with the same enthusiasm.

In the desert and on the mountains, in lonely outposts, are the graves where the bodies of these unknown soldiers lie. Sometimes the names have vanished from the wooden crosses. Sun and wind have burned them away. No one will know who these men were, and perhaps no one will ever come to their graves.

I shall never forget a man of my unit, not an outstanding figure—just a simple man among thousands of others. He was a great big German, or Austrian—I do not know which. His name was Herman. I saw him lying beside the trail which led to the besieged outpost. Men were rushing forward to the attack. I stopped beside him. Twice he had been hit. His stomach was almost open. He looked at me. He recognized me. With his eyes on mine he said:

"You are satisfied with me?"

Poor, big-hearted boy! Was I satisfied with him! . . .

It is to men of his kind that I owe it to tell the story of their hardships, of their sorrows, of their enthusiasms, of their work and play, and of all that they are called upon to do in their five years of service, which many of them prolong into ten or fifteen years, because the Legion becomes a vital part of their life. *It is their life*, and they cannot be content anywhere else!

On the flag of the French Army there are two words—*Honor and Country*. On the flag of the French Foreign Legion there are also two words— *Honor and Fidelity*. These two words express the spirit of the Legion.

BOOK I

The Bugle Sounds

I

LEGIONNAIRES IN GARRISON

Meknes

March 2, 1923

THE camp of the Legion is high above the ancient city. There were no trees here, no vegetation, when the Legion came. As everywhere else, they have made their own homes. They have planted gardens around the stone barracks. They have made roads, and planted trees along the lanes in the camp and the road that leads to the city. Life springs up wherever a legionnaire puts his foot. There was no water. So water was brought from the mountains for the trees and plants. Around the camp green shrubs were planted to hold the dust and the sand, which blows from the desert and the mountains, driving in a furious gale against all that stands in its way.

There are not many legionnaires left in camp. Most of the battalions are far away either in the

1

mountains on police duty, or constructing roads, or they are in the outposts which keep the country safe and make all progress possible.

Strangers are not aware of these outposts in the mountains. They travel in security over the country, from north to south and from east to west, seeing no soldiers, no display of arms. And they wonder how this country, which for centuries was in turmoil and strife, can be kept so quiet without an armed force.

The armed forces that are here are not here for conquest. They are unseen. Their number is not large. It is not counted in hundreds of thousands. There are only a few men, but they are reliable, they are brave, they are daring, and the consciousness of serving the good helps them to endure hardships and seclusion for the greater part of the year.

Here in Meknes are stored the supplies of the regiment. Here the tired battalions return when they are worn out, many of them barefoot and in rags. Here they are clothed anew. Here they rest, recuperate their forces, and prepare themselves to start again into the unknown.

March 3rd

How far away one feels from Europe—from civilization, here in the heart of Morocco! There is a

2

breath of mysterious Africa in the air. Crossing the country in this torrid heat, over hills and ravines completely bare, blown by the hot wind from the south, one begins to feel that he is in Africa. On either side of the road, standing high on the hills, one sees the *kasbahs* or fortified houses of the Arabs. The road passes through villages with their squares filled with natives attired in white and gray burnouses. The different mountain tribes, mingling with the Arabs and the Berbers and the Negroes brought from the Soudan by the Sultans—all this native throng makes you feel that you really are in Africa.

March 5th

Here in this ancient city one sees traces of many civilizations. The arches built by the Romans, the mosques and towers erected by the different Sultans from the eleventh to the seventeenth century, make me feel very far from Europe. I am invaded by strange, new sensations. They cannot be defined— they are different. It is all new. There is in the sun and in the soil of Africa something unique. The heat here is so penetrating. It envelops you. It clutches you. It grips your heart. The sun seems to burn through to your bones. It gets inside of you. It gives you a certain joy in living, but a joy which

3

is not boisterous, which does not manifest itself externally. It is an inner joy, a sense of tranquillity, of being at peace with yourself. This feeling becomes a part of you. It is in every nerve and fiber of your body. No one in the world can take it away from you, not even yourself.

And the nights! Here in Meknes the nights are fresh. The sky is of black velvet, and the stars glow so wonderfully. A feeling of peace comes over you. You feel lifted from the ground, as if in the midst of a vast wind of the Cosmos . . . in harmony with all the elements . . . enveloped . . . absorbed . . . transported to another sphere.

Yes, these are strange sensations. I cannot sleep at night. I go out on the terrace and give myself up to the wind that blows from the open spaces, and I have vague impressions of things that happened long ago . . . echoes from another life . . . murmurs and sighs of a world invisible and yet real, that is all encompassing. I ask myself whether in a former existence I have not lived in Africa. I do not know. But this black earth speaks to me.

The nights are superb. Never in my life have I seen a sky so full of stars, and never have they seemed so near. The starry veil of the heavens descends and covers the ancient city.

But stepping down from the terrace and going

4

into the town—what a terrible awakening! Cafés with mechanical pianos—the fox trot and tango. Through the window of a café I see women, vulgar, painted . . . soldiers . . . officers . . . civilians.

MARRAKECH
March 8th

We are now stationed in Marrakech, where there is another regiment of the Legion. What a mysterious place, Marrakech, the main southern city of Morocco. It is encircled by a wonderful border of palm trees, while to the south the snowy walls of the Great Atlas bar the road to the desert. When I go to the city, which is four miles distant from the camp, I like to watch the chains of white and rose mountains, bathed by the multicolored rays of the African sun. For there is a special African sun which is of incredible magnificence. I have observed that the sun as well as the sky gives you different emotions on different continents. Here in Africa I experience a very real and strange emotion every morning when the sun comes up; and in the evening, when the sun touches the horizon, a certain sadness overtakes the heart—perhaps it is the fear that there may not be another day so luminous.

This evening I am going to a square in the city, Djemaa el Fna (The Assembly of the Follies), an

5

immense place that has no form. One cannot say whether it is round, or oval, or square, or long, because of the multitude of people who fill it. They are dressed in white and gray and black burnouses with turbans of various shapes. Each one wears his turban in his own particular way. Then there are also multitudes of dancers, clowns, fire-swallowers, singers, story-tellers and snake charmers. There are venders of fruit. There are criers of all kinds of articles. . . . Oh, the cries, the chants, the music— tambourines, pipers, violins—oh, this *hua, hua, hua!*

Turning to the west I see the sky intensely red, and against the horizon an old mosque, and above the mosque the ancient Tower of Koutoubia. . . . No, no, one has to see this scene in order to appreciate it—to feel this life which is so different, this life which is so intense, yet so contemplative and calm.

March 10th

Yesterday I went with another officer of the Legion to the city. I have found in him a really superior soul. He has been commanding in the Legion for the last fifteen years—an excellent officer and chief, very calm, a man who has a rich and intense inner life. We left our horses with our orderlies at the entrance to the Arab quarter. We

6

walked through the streets and alleys with their bazaars and shops. Each trade has its own section in the native street. Here are blacksmiths, there are saddlemakers, and still further along are carpenters, basketmakers and other artisans. And how they work! These are not the workingmen of factories who run machines. They are artists who create everything with their own hands. They have intelligent faces, these simple people, and what wisdom is inscribed on their attentive figures while they work. I have noticed in general that the man with a task always looks beautiful, even if his features are not beautiful. There is a certain spirituality which radiates from people who work, who are obliged to work. Work of any kind ennobles a human being.

March 11th

The sun is very hot to-day. We remained in the field all this afternoon to see the newly promoted corporals maneuver. Of these new noncommissioned officers, one is an Italian, one Spanish, one Polish, one Moroccan, four are French, three Russian, two Swiss, and about ten are German. This is an organization of international troops. A man, no matter what his nationality, who enters this corps of troops, becomes in a very short time a legionnaire and a legionnaire only.

7

There always have been Germans in the Legion since it was founded about one hundred years ago.

When Alsace and Lorraine were annexed by Germany, the men of these provinces, not wishing to serve in the German Army, deserted and came over to serve in the Foreign Legion, and after five years of service, many asked to be naturalized and become French. But also men from Bavaria, Prussia, Mecklenburg and other German provinces continued to come as before.

Prior to the Great War the Germans in the Legion numbered not more than 20 per cent, but after the War Germans and Russians predominated. The Germans formed 50 per cent of the Legion and were the more stable element. Most of them had served in their own army during the Great War. Some of them were Spartacists and joined the Legion when that movement was put down in Germany. Many were members of the other extreme, belonging to the ultra-Monarchist party. They came to the Legion not wanting to serve the German Republic. These two opposite groups met there, clad in the French Foreign Legion uniform, and lived in the same squad, the same group, the same section. They were different in type and education. While the Monarchists were ex-Prussian officers, men of the nobility or professional soldiers of the Prussian

8

Army, in the Spartacist group were intellectuals, schoolmasters, students, engineers and workingmen.

There were very few Russians in the Legion before the War. They came to the Legion after the defeat of the White Movement in Russia. After the evacuation of General Denikin's forces of Novorossijsk in 1919 and the evacuation by General Wrangel's Army of Sebastopol in 1920, the men of the White Army found themselves in a most fearful plight when they were brought to Constantinople. Thousands of them then enlisted in the Legion. They were chiefly soldiers, many of them Cossacks from the Don and from the Kouban. This Russian element in the Foreign Legion is probably only a casual one. At the expiration of their five years' service the majority of them will leave and look for civil occupations in France and elsewhere. Their number will gradually diminish. Not many of them will return to Russia, because they still fear persecution on the part of the present Soviet Government. And then their relatives in Russia are not very eager to have them come back.

My orderly, who is a Cossack from Kouban, once said to me bitterly:

"I write to my brother asking him what are the conditions there and whether I could come, and this is what I receive." He had a letter in his hand. "He

9

says, 'Don't come.' I have not seen him for eight years and I would suppose that a brother might be glad to receive me after so many years of suffering. 'No,' he says, 'no, don't come. Times are bad.' But I know that they aren't having such bad times there. They have recovered all their land—they have even more land than they had before—and I know from another relative that the number of their cattle has also increased. So they could have room for me. But no, he doesn't want me to come, because he thinks that I may claim my part in the family property—my piece of land. Well, let them have it. I won't go back."

I asked him whether many of his comrades, Russians, are in the same position in relation to their people in Russia.

He said, "Oh, yes, many of them—most of them—are in the same position."

The sergeants and corporals in the Legion are mostly Germans, and Germans especially make good corporals. Russians do not make good corporals because the Russian is always hesitating, and somehow he does not have authority over the men with whom he is living and sharing the same room or tent. He hesitates when he commands. He is not firm. He is lenient, and not sure of his authority. The tone of his voice is not convincing, and even

10

while ordering them to do this or that, he seems to doubt as to whether they really must do it. But the German, immediately after he is invested with the rank of corporal and the two green stripes are sewn on his sleeve, feels himself a chief and a commander. And he commands his men. He has charge of eight, twelve or sixteen, or whatever number are placed under his immediate command. He will make them obey his orders, and although eating with them from the same plate and sleeping beside them, he will always make them feel that he is their chief. Although these German corporals get just as drunk as their men, a German corporal never drinks with the men of his squad or of his group.

But the Germans, although excellent corporals, do not always make good sergeants. If Germans only were under them it would be all right, but they have men of other nationalities, other races, under their command, and the German methods which they want to apply do not work with the others. They also lack a knowledge of psychology. Only those who have been a long time in the Legion change their methods. It is our duty to instruct them, to supervise them, and to make them understand other ways of managing men.

The Russian sergeant, being very attentive to the men, very scrupulous in all his actions, but lacking

11

energy, has to be urged to be more severe and authoritative, while on the other hand, restrain the German sergeant from being too brutal to his men.

However, in the long run, Germans or Russians, men of Latin races, or others, after two or three years in the service are all shaped according to the long-established traditions of the Legion.

Strange as it may seem, the most sober element in the Legion after the War was Russian. They very seldom drank. They were very quiet and most obedient. Perhaps it was because every one of them had the idea, after finishing his five years of service, of going hence and starting a new life. Among the Russians there are men who, even out of the small pay of the French soldier, save up money. I know a dozen cases where the Russian legionnaires give to their captains every fortnight a few francs to save for them against the day of their liberation, and many of them have saved up two or three hundred francs. But the others, especially the Germans, never dream of saving money. They all drink heavily, and while generally obedient, for a few days after they receive their pay they become the most riotous element in the ranks. While the Italian or Spaniard usually drinks quietly alone his glass or his bottle of wine, the Germans drink in groups and incite one another to some scandalous action. But

12

they are brave in battle; and, on the whole, are the most reliable men of the Legion.

March 13th

All is quiet in my room. The sun is down. What calm reigns in the camp! After the day's work is ended the legionnaires are allowed to go to the city, three miles away. The officers have already gone there. Only a few orderlies remain to straighten up the rooms, and soon they will leave. In a few minutes I shall dress and go away also. Every evening carriages are waiting at the entrance of the camp to take us to the city. On the road I pass soldiers on leave, Moroccans, Algerians, Senegalese, legionnaires—all going down to spend a few hours in the cafés and native quarter of the city.

Night of the Same Day

More and more I enjoy life with the troops. One is near the men. There is direct action and influence over human beings. Every unit is a reflection of the chief who commands it. But one has to know how to command. . . . One of my lieutenants has seen about twenty years of service. He knows his profession wonderfully. There is also a young graduate from Saint Cyr, very nervous, but an excellent officer. He takes great interest in tennis and danc-

13

ing. He rides admirably. He needs to be more calm with the men and less nervous.

For a long time I have not felt so happy and so in love with life as I do now. When from my camp I pass through the plowed fields to go to Menara, the ancient park of the Sultans, with its groves of olive and orange trees, my heart sings. Every morning when I mount my horse I bless the sky which covers me and the sun which warms me. I am becoming a pagan, because I adore with a most passionate love the elements of nature, which I think of as Beings one could adore.

How delightful it is to allow oneself to be swayed by the measured pace of a horse passing along a road lined with olive trees! Looking through the green foliage, the blue of the sky seems liquid, bathing and enveloping the branches and trunks of the trees.

There is an impressive calm in this park. Almost always I am alone. The birds are chanting their song of spring. I dismount. A little Arab boy, the son of the keeper of the park, comes and takes my horse. There is an artificial pool more than one hundred yards long, the sky reflected in its clear waters. The pool has a frame of gray stone. I stop and listen to the silence, to the complete calm. I do not know how many minutes or hours I remain.

14

Time has another pace here. Then I mount my horse and regret I have to leave. I take another road back to camp, riding beside the ancient walls which were built centuries ago, and which have seen other riders of other times.

March 14th

This is our last day at Marrakech. To-morrow at sunrise we go away. Kasbah Tadla is the place where we will take garrison for a year. We are told that it is very ugly and not at all interesting. Fortunately, we have about six months' campaigning before us. I shall always cherish the memory of my stay in Marrakech, a city full of interest, charm and beauty. For a week we shall be on the road covering from thirty to forty kilometers a day, cut off from the entire world with only two platoons of Spahis in the midst of this African country.

II

ON THE ROAD

En Route
March 15, 1923

I REGRETTED to leave Marrakech, but here on the road, marching always ahead into the unknown, one forgets everything. One is absorbed by new thoughts, that develop gradually as one advances.

March 17th

Here is our third bivouac. The first and second days we were roasted by the sun. We are quite black. We left Marrakech before sunrise. When the bugle sounded for reveille it was still dark. The night was cold; the sky of indescribable beauty. As the battalion assembled the men seemed like so many shadows passing over the grass. It was still dark when the morning star appeared on the horizon, so wonderful and gleaming. The east began to grow lighter, then the rest of the sky, and slowly this brightness, this clarity, spread over all the heavens.

A whistle, and we were on the road again. The

road turned northeast. At first the mountains were crimson, then as the sky became lighter, there was a rapid change to the most varied colors. . . .

To-day's was the third sunrise on our march, and each time it was different. One is never tired of seeing it again and again, or of starting each day to march toward the east to meet the sun. I am feeling it still in me since this morning—the sun. I am writing this in the evening in my tent. It is damp; it rains. It is cold, and the sky is covered. Half of my tent flap is open, and through it I can see other tents, horses, mules, men rushing on different errands, and still farther back a forest of trees, then hills, and in the far distance the rocky mountains toward which we are driving.

March 19th

Forty kilometers to-day! The wind was very strong. The men marched singing all the time— every one in his own mother tongue. The dust covered us, and it was difficult to advance. It is not more than two hours since we reached the camp, but already everything is in order.

Immediately upon our arrival here the Caid of the district, whose kasbah one can see from very far away, came to present his compliments to the chief of our detachment, and he invited all the officers to

17

his house. We went just as we were, covered with dust and blackened by the sun. These chateaux are really medieval fortresses. The Caid, surrounded by his relatives, his friends, his clients, his servants and his slaves, met us at the entrance and showed us to the interior. Everything was severe here, like the rocks among which these people live.

A repast was offered us. Dancers came in and entertained us.

We returned to the camp when it was almost dark. The men, tired from their day's march, were quiet in their tents. Soon the bugler will sound taps, then the whole camp will be plunged in darkness, and only the vigilant sentries will be stirring through the night.

A sweet and penetrating calm spreads over one's soul. At sunrise we will start once more on the road.

March 24th

To-morrow we shall be in Kasbah Tadla. We have not been altogether favored by the weather. Rain began to fall one afternoon and did not stop until the following day in the evening. Men, officers and animals were wet to the skin. My tent was invaded by water, and I slept, all dressed, and shivered with the cold and dampness. But the sun is a superb physician. It cures everything. Yesterday and to-day the weather is wonderful again. The rays of the sun burn our faces, and bring vigor and energy.

KASBAH TADLA
March 25th

The Colonel of our regiment came here to see us. He brought us instructions for the approaching campaign. We are to stay only one day and a half in Tadla, and then we are going into the mountains.

For some time the inhabitants of the villages on the rich plain of Tadla have been suffering from incursions of brigands, who, under cover of night, come from the mountains to raid the people. The peasants in these villages became much alarmed and were abandoning their homes. The friendly tribes living in the vicinity armed themselves, and they have appealed to us for help.

We are to go with them into the mountains. We shall press with our forces against the mountain tribes, who for centuries have lived by loot and pillage. We shall endeavor to treat with them and induce them to labor and live in peace, as so many other tribes have done during the past ten years. Perhaps we shall meet with resistance. Or perhaps,

19

seeing our strength, they will treat with us, and we shall build our outpost.

Then around this advanced post, protected by our neutral forces, they will settle peacefully their grievances. Perhaps they will ask to have a fight of honor, to be fought between them and the tribes of the plains. A day will be set for the fighting. There will be much shooting and shouting from dawn to sunset. There will be a few killed and wounded. After this the different tribes will come together, and celebrate their reconciliation by a fête lasting several days. Then they will begin to help construct our outposts in order to make these friendly relations between the tribes permanent.

Night of the Same Day

We are camping above the town of Kasbah Tadla, on a plateau on the bank of the river Oum el Rhebia, whose troubled waters flow swiftly from the mountains. It is crossed by a bridge the Portuguese built centuries ago. The plateau overlooks the town, which at one time was all inside the high battlemented walls of the kasbah. Kasbah Tadla was one of the greatest strongholds of the Sultans of Morocco. Almost destroyed, and abandoned for centuries, changing hands many times, its possession disputed by one chief or another, it has led a weary and miserable life. The rich and prosperous plains which flourished under the rule of the powerful Sultans of the seventeenth century were left uncultivated and forsaken. It is only during the past ten years that an era of prosperity has come back to these plains of ancient Numidia.

Under the protection of our outposts a peaceful life is now possible. The natives have begun to cultivate the fields and a new town has been built up around the kasbah. Highways have been made —one running from Tadla to Casablanca, more than two hundred miles distant. Before our arrival it was almost beyond the imagination of man to go to this distant city. And those who went there were considered by the population to have done something remarkable. They were looked upon with awe and with respect.

Now the native takes a big motor truck. He loads it with his produce, and goes to the market of the great city with its hundred thousand population, its magnificent buildings, its port. He returns bewildered from this trip, and spreads the news among his people of the wonderful life he has seen. Traveling on a donkey's back for an entire day to go to a market twenty miles distant and traveling two hundred miles in six hours in an automobile are so amazingly different as to be almost unbelievable.

21

DECHRA EL OUED
March 26th

Instead of leaving Kasbah Tadla at sunrise, we left our camp about eleven o'clock in the morning, starting on the road when the sun was already high above our heads. There are those among us that will never see the blue sky again!

Morocco is a cold country where the sun is hot. The difference in temperature between day and night is very great. There is the same difference between a day when the sun shines and a dark day full of clouds. In the month of March great storms sweep over the country. One must not trust the sun. Before a storm it becomes very hot and the air is so heavy one can hardly breathe. Yet we march on, no matter how trying it is. And sometimes we have to pay heavily for it: we have two dead from sunstroke and several soldiers are on stretchers in the field ambulances. Poor men! I have seen one of them dying. . . . In my company every man is safe. I did not allow anyone to leave the ranks and drink water from the streams that ran alongside the road. It brings fever. . . .

The heat became more and more excessive. I needed to cover my neck with a scarf, but seeing my men loaded down with their heavy packs, their rifles, two heavy water bottles and 120 cartridges in their

22

cartridge belts, marching afoot, I was ashamed, being mounted, to be covered more than they were.

Anougal

March 29th

We are now in the heart of the mountains where dwell the tribes which we are here to pacify. The operations began at six o'clock in the morning. To-day we are in the rear guard, not only of the battalion, but of all the troops, protected by a platoon of cavalry.

The morning was very tempestuous and rain began to fall about two o'clock in the afternoon. The battery of 75's and the carts were in a tangled mass in the ravine with no possibility of going ahead. The engineers have been trying their best to make a road, but the rain has transformed the ground into a morass, and the horses and mules and the poor men moved with the greatest difficulty. We were left alone in a mountain pass. The chief of the detachment, unaware of our difficulties, had pushed forward. Fearing an attack, I placed my men on both sides of the ravine, occupying the most salient points, from which I could observe the country around and defend the convoy, if necessary. The rain was icy and we were wet through.

One can imagine in what condition my men

23

reached the camp. Although it was dark already, we had still to make our trenches for the night, and under continued rain. This night no one will sleep. No tents can be set up in this deep mud. Nevertheless, the men succeeded in starting fires and in drying themselves. Every time, after a big effort has been made by the men, and they finally reach the camp, they forget the hardships, and their morale is wonderful. I see them around the fire talking and even singing.

The mountain we are occupying is our first objective. An outpost has to be built here at Anougal to command the passes in this part of the country and to close to the hostile tribes the road to the valley, in order to make it safe for those who live there. The country seems deserted. There is nobody in sight. Not a shot has been fired. Our only losses are the two men who died from sunstroke.

III

CONSTRUCTING OUTPOSTS

Koomsh

April 1, 1923

IT took only two days for the weather to change completely. A few days ago men were falling from sunstroke, but when we entered the mountains we were in the midst of winter.

Leaving one battalion of the Legion at Anougal, we went deeper into the mountains, now climbing steep heights, now descending abruptly. Finally we came to a richly cultivated valley, where the villages had been abandoned by their inhabitants.

This enchanted valley is shut in on both sides by high mountains. It was not raining when we arrived, but there were thick clouds above our heads and a heavy mist enveloped everything. We camped there for a few hours. The commanders of the different units were ordered to climb the highest peaks in order to reconnoiter and find a place where we could camp. We were to remain there for about ten days. During this time we must construct an-

25

other outpost, that of Koomsh, which would command all the country around and which would close other accesses to the valley of Tadla. As soon as the place had been chosen, some of the men were given axes to cut down the trees. Others with hammers and picks were to break the rocks and clear the ground that the tents might be pitched.

The crest of the mountain was thickly wooded, and in order to have a clear view of the ground around the camp, we had to cut down trees that stood there like a wall. Gangs of men started to work, and soon all this dormant place, where never before a white man had come, echoed with hundreds of sounds.

A road had to be made to bring up the guns, mules, horses and men. The installation of a battalion of infantry of the Legion, of a squadron of cavalry, of a battery of four guns, and all the convoy, took a long time. It was dark when everybody reached the top.

Then again the rain started to fall. Torrents of waters descended on us, and made the ground like jelly. There on this soft earth the men had to pitch their tents, and there they had to lie down. The officers fared no better. I remained all night outside to see how my men were situated, and to see how the sentries and the machine guns were placed.

Some of the men worked through the night putting up barbed-wire defenses, while others built a stone wall to protect us from bullets in case of attack. All the night the rain did not stop. It grew cooler and cooler, and before dawn snow had whitened all the slopes of the mountains and also our tents.

During the morning the snow continued to fall. Nevertheless the work had to be done. Gangs of men went to work—masons, stone-breakers, miners who drilled the rocks in order to dynamite them, men with picks and shovels who traced the outline of the post. Other men with picks and shovels chose an appropriate place, and then dug holes in the ground to make limekilns; others cut down more trees for firewood to feed the ovens, where stone was being transformed into lime. Every one had his task. The muleteers, protected by a platoon of Spahis, took their animals to water at the creek that ran below the camp. The camp was alive. This canvas town, just created, was busy and active. Camp fires were started and food was prepared for the men. Early in the afternoon a convoy had to leave for the rear, to go to a base established in an old kasbah in the foothills. Food had to be brought, and at the same time a survey of the country must be made, in order to find a place where a road could

27

be built eventually to connect future outposts with the rear.

April 4th

We are the pioneers who open a new country. We are the rugged, primitive laborers who do the hardest work. We are the visionaries who see wonderful possibilities in the future. After the Legion, other men will come. These men will be praised. Their names will be known. But it is our men of the Legion who have paved the way with their untiring labor. Every path we make bears the pain of our men. It is they who have opened the way for civilization to come into the heart of this savage country. I like this primitive life. I feel so strong and gay. I feel in communion with my men.

April 6th

Food supplies come regularly, and the men are well fed. When I go to the camp kitchens to taste the food prepared for them I always think that I would rather have their food than that prepared for the officers' mess. The first thing in the morning, when the men awaken, they have a cup of coffee. Two mornings in the week they have coffee and milk, or cocoa. At eight o'clock a *casse croûte* is given to them, consisting of cheese and bread, sausage and bread, or sardines. At eleven o'clock they have a full pail of soup, thick with vegetables, meat with potatoes, or beans, or rice, or macaroni, and a quart of red wine, and coffee. At three o'clock hot tea is brought to the workers. And finally, in the evening, they have another full meal.

There is always plenty of bread, more than the legionnaires can eat. Bread, coffee, sugar, salt, beans, rice and wine are delivered to the units gratuitously by the commissariat of the army. It also provides for live stock to be butchered, or it sends fresh meat, if the post is near and accessible, and if the weather is not too hot. In addition to all this, a sum of money for each man is put in the possession of the captain, who spends it on food for his men. With economy and by careful planning he is able to buy jam, cheese, chocolate, fresh vegetables and, which the legionnaires like best of all, additional rations of wine.

April 10th

We have had an extremely hard day. From morning until night we were forced to remain outside under continuous rain. The men are tired; they begin to be irritable. We are certain to have sickness.

In the evening the sergeant major came to my

tent with a report of the happenings of the day. One man had gotten drunk and insulted a sergeant. Another had menaced the sentry with a pick. A third one had left the work without authorization. A fourth was late to the assembly of the company. And so on.

One of my lieutenants has been in bed since yesterday with fever. Another was hit in the face by a stone when some rocks were blown up, and he also remains in his tent.

It is a peculiar life—this life of an officer with his troops. One who has never tried it cannot know what it means.

April 11th

After so many days of rain, the sun came out for a few minutes while the men were working. Only to hear the cries, the shouts of joy, from the hundreds of men who for the last week have slept on the wet ground after a hard day's work!

April 12th

Since this morning the weather has changed completely. After the bugle had sounded reveille at five o'clock, my orderly came to open the tent and bring my coffee. How solemn he was! His voice trembled, and he even had tears in his eyes when

30

he announced, "The sky is clear. There will be sun."

To-day has been marvelous. What an amount of work has been done by the men! They had to construct the southeast side of the fortress. I glowed with pride when I saw the cornerstones of the wall rising above the ground. And as the walls began to rise one could visualize the outlines of the future post. Complete absorption in work—what other joy equals it!

I feel a great inner elation. How can I express this feeling so warm and so intimate—this feeling of joy and love which comes over me without any apparent reason when nothing has happened to justify it. I try to hide it within myself, because if I were to express it to some of the people who are around me they would not understand. When I was with my men, the rain pouring down, and I saw how they forgot themselves in their work, my heart was filled with admiration for them.

April 13th

An accident has happened to-day. Two men have had their heads broken by a large stone that fell upon them. Every day we blow up certain sections. The work continues, and the walls of the post are rising with extraordinary rapidity.

31

The work of a mason is fascinating. Here lies a heap of stones, in disorder, with no form, and apparently useless; but the same stones become useful in the hands of a mason who knows how to build. He scrutinizes the material, and discerns in this formless mass the shape and the quality that he needs for building.

It is the same with men. Millions and millions do not know themselves. They are useless to themselves and to others. But the time comes when a master builder has need for material, and he shapes this mass, untried and formless, in the interest of some great achievement. If one has an ideal, a general conception of what one wants, the material always can be found. We are all of us in the service of a superior force, and we only need to know and to feel our vocation.

Life will become wonderful when men finally realize the oneness of the human race, when all humanity will live as one harmonious whole. It is only through labor and effort that the darkness of ignorance, hatred and division will disappear. And it is only through work that mankind will be purified and raised from its narrow egotism.

Here is a group of men representing twenty different nationalities which have been separated by enmities and strife. A common aim is given them, a useful piece of work set before them, and at once they become brothers in arms and companions in work.

April 14th

It is still dark. The sun has not risen. The wind is blowing, and from its glacial breath it seems as if once more it would bring snow or a very cold rain. At three o'clock I walked out of my tent to make the rounds of the sentry posts. It was dark . . . dark . . . and I could not even see the rocky ground over which I had to make my way.

I like these nights, so mysterious and full of the unknown. Night, just as death, brings men closer, one to another.

When one stops near a sentry, just before reaching him, he cries out into the night, "Halt! Who goes there!" Instinctively one stops and a shiver passes over one's body. One approaches the man who, notwithstanding the great cold, stands still at his post, piercing with his eyes the silence and the darkness of the night. One comes near to him and says, "It is cold, *mon ami.*" He answers in a low voice, "Yes, but it doesn't matter." And he puts into this simple phrase such a warmth of tone that I feel close to him.

I have always liked this hour of making the

rounds. The silence of the night is so complex. One hears the breathing of hundreds of men asleep in their tents. One hears the animals sleeping on their feet and pawing the ground and sighing deeply and loudly.

And then the forest, that covers the tops of the mountains, wakened by the wind, begins to murmur, to sing, to whistle. The forest is like a sea, and sometimes forgetting where I am, I feel myself transported to the borders of far-away waters. Yes, I like these nights when I am on the rounds, even if the weather is terrible. The depth of my heart is opened, and I hear strange calls. I do not know from whence they come. I cannot define them. They come from some obscure source.

*   *   *   *   *

Before entering my tent I stop in front of the assistant cook. Half frozen with the cold, he is endeavoring, with great difficulty, to start a fire in order to prepare coffee for the men, who will be awakened within a short time, and who immediately after being awakened, half asleep yet, will clamor for the hot liquid. This assistant cook is a volunteer for the job.

"I don't sleep at night," he says, "I might as well be doing this. I am afraid to go to sleep."

He looks into the flames. With a long stick he

stirs the fire and hundreds of sparks flash out and disappear into the darkness. He is silent for a moment, and then he begins to talk again.

"When I was little, my mother said to me, 'Jean, don't tell lies. If once you tell a lie, God will punish you. If you close your eyes for the night, God will not open them in the morning any more. You will die!' And when after that I told a lie, immediately I became frightened. I was terrified for fear of punishment by the *bon Dieu*. On the night of my first lie I remained awake, and in order not to close my eyes, I held the lids open with my hands. Since then I have lied many times, and have not been punished. One day, when I was yet young, I lied wantonly to defy God. I said to myself, 'Here! I stand before you! I will lie!' And at night I closed my eyes to see if I would be able to open them in the morning—if God would strike me with death. I thought I should die, but nothing happened. Thinking of death, I already pitied myself. Also I rejoiced in the fact that my parents would have sorrow. I was bitter toward my parents then, you see. . . ."

He fell silent again. He took off the kettle of boiling water, threw handfuls of coffee into it, and placed it over the fire. He threw more wood on the

35

fire, and put another receptacle of water over the flame.

"There are men who come and ask for hot water to wash up," he said. "I always have some for them."

Then, after a long pause, he went on: "No, I can't sleep. I hate night! I am horrified at the idea that I may die in the night—that death may come as a thief, and steal me away. Death! I want to see it with my eyes . . . straight before me . . . struggle with it . . . defy it. . . . I don't want to be surprised by it. It is different in battle. There one is fighting . . . struggling . . . one is facing it. Then I have no fear, because I can measure myself against it. But at nighttime . . . no. You see, I cannot go to sleep, and I prefer to start the fire and watch the flames going out in the air, piercing the darkness. . . ."

April 15th

To-morrow we leave Koomsh. The outpost is built, and it is a great satisfaction to see the place absolutely transformed. Instead of a mass of rock thrown here chaotically by nature, the ground is leveled, roads and trails are cut, and the post itself stands forth on the height of the mountain to signal welcome to every one who may need refuge.

Notwithstanding the great trials of the bad weather, everybody has borne up remarkably well, and that is because the men have been occupied with work. If we had allowed them to lie down under their tents in the dampness and cold, they would perhaps all be dead by now. But everybody has worked, and that has saved us.

A captain of the Colonial Regiment and fifty Senegalese soldiers are installed here. Foodstuffs have been brought, enough to last for three months, and every fifteen days a courier will come to bring mail and news from the outside world. A telephone line has been established, but one cannot count on it, because it may be cut by brigands.

April 16th

The sun is hot to-day, hotter than ever. We left the mountain at daybreak, and camped in the valley at the foot of the post. At one o'clock, after midday, we broke camp. We came down by a trail winding through plowed and sown fields, and stretches of land full of high, juicy grass and wild flowers of the most wonderful colors—marguerites, flowers blue and yellow and red, and other hues I never shall be able to describe because of their infinite variety.

Yes, the sun was hot and the men, who have not marched for more than fifteen days, and who are badly shod, walked with great difficulty. They struggled along painfully. Many of them fell exhausted by the roadside. A rear guard was detailed to pick up those who were tired, and help them to reach the halting place. Many of the men carried the packs of their weaker comrades. One man dropped dead. He got drunk last night, and to-day the sun of Africa has knocked him out.

KSIBA
April 17th

We are camping on a plateau, facing the large native village of Ksiba which is surrounded by walls. There in the kasbah lives Caid Ali, a young Berber, who came from the mountains with a few hundred families of his tribe to submit himself to the French Protectorate. His old father, the big chief of the region, and the one most feared by his neighbors, has not yet yielded to the Central Government of Morocco, and leads a semi-nomadic life in the mountains.

We had a most disturbing night. Our camp was attacked by a band of brigands. There was shooting from all sides. One legionnaire of my company,

38

Velich, was badly wounded. He died this morning. Two rifles were taken from a tent; near by a dagger was found, and still farther on an old burnous, with another dagger. Nobody in the tent was assassinated.

Poor young Velich, a good Serbian boy, was our best machine gunner. He was carried to the nearest outpost, and buried there in the cemetery, where other legionnaires are resting. The lieutenant of his section, speaking at his grave, said:

"In the name of the company I salute most humbly and respectfully the mortal remains of our dear comrade in battle, Velich. He has been taken away from us in his fourth year of service in Morocco. He was killed by brigands while doing his duty. Velich died on the field of honor. In the new life that he is entering, in the Great Eternity, Velich will be just as great as he was here on earth, where he kept his word as a legionnaire and died under the flag of the Legion which bears these words, 'Valor and Discipline,' 'Honor and Fidelity.' Adieu, Velich, rest in peace. The company promises that it will never forget you."

What a strange life one leads here with the legionnaires! How sensitive they are, and how they react to everything! Last night a storm came up. I

walked out to make my rounds. The first quarter of
the moon was already in the west, and around it was
a white circle which gradually spread over the sky.
Clouds were coming from the south.

A legionnaire—a Russian Tartar—serving as
sentry on the southern watch tower, said when I came
to him, "There will be rain soon."

And about two o'clock in the morning the rain was
pouring down. It seemed as if it would never stop.
There was a terrible wind all day long, but after
sunset everything became quiet, and there was a
sweetness in the air from the grass and flowers,
brought by the light wind blowing from the hills
and the valleys. And faintly one heard the sound
of the flowing river.

The men sang for a long time last night. After
they experience some excitement, or surmount some
difficulty—when it is all over, their souls require some
harmony and rhythm. Last evening they sang especially well. The Germans have a very sentimental
song called "The Old Village Schoolmaster," into
whose simple words they put genuine emotion.

When they sing there is a far-away look in the
eyes of these men; they are seeing farther than this
outpost, farther than these valleys, even beyond
these most distant mountains. Then came a song in
French which the legionnaires composed themselves:

40

In Morocco where the sun is breathing with heat,
Lonely stands a legionnaire,
He stands still on the rocks
And holds tightly his rifle.
He holds his rifle.
He nods his head sadly and thinks
Of his country.

The Russians sang too. Their songs and choruses are more complex than the songs of the Germans.

The French cannot sing in chorus. There are individuals among them who sing well, though, and they are very good story-tellers.

On these nights the native troops who are living in the annex of the post come within the walls of our courtyard to listen to the songs of these light-haired men from the north.

PLATEAU OF IFREN
April 18th

Instead of going for a rest to Kasbah Tadla orders came to occupy another mountain, Ifren, and to construct a blockhouse there. Caid Ali's men are to occupy this fortification when it is finished, and they will defend the country from other factions of their tribe, with whom they have not yet settled their differences.

41

The men, who had not slept last night on account of the skirmish with brigands, worked until late into the night to entrench themselves and to erect a wall, almost as high as a man, around the front of the unit.

To-night nothing happened. It was calm. The nightingales were singing marvelously. I was sleepless. The occurrences of last night weighed upon me still. I was thinking of my young legionnaire, Velich. His blood running in a stream. . . . He was lying down on the ground. . . . A Russian gave him first aid, while the fusillade was going on. He did not open his eyes. When I last saw him his face was peaceful. There was in his expression the grandeur of the soldier who dies on duty. . . .

Only three days to construct the blockhouse. The weather is so bad . . . how are we going to do it?

April 19th

A great storm has been driving through the mountains. Hail and snow succeeded each other. And one blast of the wind has carried away my tent. Again cold, as in the winter. And we are clothed for summer weather. Our men did not go to work until midday. They were left to rest. In the afternoon they left their tents and started to work, but could not proceed with it. They were absolutely drenched. Many have fever. It will be hard to build the blockhouse. Two hundred mules carrying sacks of lime have just come to the camp. The muleteers and the animals are exhausted! The trails have been absolutely impassable. We cannot send the mules back. Food will be lacking, and we shall have to consume our reserve stores, which will not last more than two days. The men are in rags.

April 20th

A letter arrived to-day from a comrade who is commanding a battalion of the Legion. His unit is also in the mountains, operating in the region of Taza.

"I always thought there was much exaggeration when officers of the Legion talked about their men," he writes. "Why should the legionnaires be any better than other troops? I didn't quite believe the legend. But a few months in command of a detachment of the Legion has convinced me of its truth.

"You cannot imagine the endurance of our young legionnaires. We are now in a country which is absolutely awful to travel through: bare rocks and nothing else. And the sun is terribly hot. In addition to that, damnable snipers are hidden among the rocks and do us great damage. We are now in the

43

'pocket of Taza' with the most redoubtable tribes on all sides. . . .

"Last week General Poeymireau came to visit us —just to spend a day with the Legion, he said. The men knew and admired him. They surpassed themselves while he stayed among us. They danced, they sang, they played. . . . What a beautiful face he has, this young general! I understand now why the *Maréchal* has succeeded in Morocco! He surrounded himself with young and talented men. Those here in Morocco are idealists and enthusiasts.

"General Poeymireau decorated a few men of my battalion. There was an enormously tall Dane in the ranks. When the General pinned the war cross on his breast the giant almost cried with emotion. Poeymireau said to him:

" 'You are a brave fellow, *mon petit*. Do you understand?'

" '*Moi comprise*,' said the '*petit*' giant Dane, with tears in his eyes.

"In a month we shall be through with the operations here. We shall pacify completely the region and the road to Algiers will be safe. . . .''

One more day goes by! The bad weather continues. All night the rain and the snow did not cease. This morning it was difficult to assemble the

44

companies and conduct them to work. The men are unhappy. They shiver—their clothes are never dry. But the work has to be finished. There is only food for two days, and everybody will be sick. There are eight sick to-day. The noncommissioned officers are also exhausted. I assembled the company and said to them:

"The difficulties are great. I am aware of it. No other troops have to endure what you endure. It has always been so with the Legion. Sun and rain and cold have been against us. But with two days more of great effort, our work will be completed."

I congratulated all my men and the corporals and sergeants particularly on the way in which they have accomplished their task under such difficult conditions. I made an appeal to the spirit of abnegation, initiative and sacrifice of the whole Legion.

Are the hardships endured by the troops of occupation in Morocco known to the outside world? Seen from afar, from Paris, or even from a big city in Morocco, can people realize all that these troops suffer? Can it be imagined by those who have not lived through it? There are many military men with easy jobs who remain in the cities, and know nothing of the hardships of the campaign.

To-night . . . another alarm! The sentries

opened fire, but everything became quiet in a few minutes. I did not close my eyes, and it seemed to me, several times, that somebody was crawling on the ground near my tent.

April 21st

At last the weather is getting better. The block-house is almost done. To-morrow we shall go away. These were the orders for the morning:

"To-morrow reveille at five o'clock. Beginning of work five-thirty. The morning meal will be consumed as soon as the post is finished. We shall break camp immediately after eating. The detachment will leave the place in the direction of Kasbah Tadla, where it will arrive in the evening, if the condition of the trails and the physical state of the troops permit."

En Route
April 22nd

We bivouac twelve kilometers from Kasbah Tadla. A quiet night of rest. This morning we had rain. Soon it will clear up. At midday, when we left the camp, one could already see the superb blue of the African sky. Our men of the Legion are really aces. Many of them have no shoes, and they march barefoot. Many are sick. Notwith-

46

standing that, everybody goes ahead. There are a few men who cannot keep up the pace, but, on the whole, everybody marches well. The month of rain and extreme cold has been a great experience for troops equipped only with protection from sun and heat. The commander of the region has sent ten wagons to meet us, in order to bring in those who cannot walk, but not one legionnaire of the battalion has taken a place in the wagons and we have sent them away.

KASBAH TADLA
April 23rd

Finally we reached Tadla. All the garrison came out to meet us. The music of the regiment greeted us half a mile from the town. The inhabitants were in the main street leading to the camp. They thought we would arrive half-dead from fatigue, and they were surprised to see us marching in perfect order.

Felicitations were issued to the detachment. The men will have two days of rest and quiet, and a supplementary quart of white wine every day.

IV

QUIET LIFE IN KASBAH TADLA

Kasbah Tadla
April 28, 1923

THE men are glad to be in Tadla. They need to recuperate. They need an opportunity to clean themselves up—to have good food, and nights of sleep and rest. All their clothing has to be renewed. The legionnaire likes to look clean, trim and smart. Here in Tadla they meet legionnaires of other battalions. They always like to see one another, these brothers in arms. Many of them have met before; many meet now for the first time. Chatting over a bottle of wine, they discover men of their own nationality. They find that they have mutual friends in their own countries. They revive memories of their former life. They tell one another stories of their exploits and recall hardships undergone during campaigns. They even tell of events that never happened. Sitting there, they give free rein to their imagination.

On the day that they receive their meager pay,

48

they fill up all the cafés in the small town. The main street contains almost nothing but cafés. There the legionnaire dances to the music of mechanical pianos—his kepi over one ear, his tunic unbuttoned, a cigarette in the corner of his mouth.

Half drunk, he is still filled with the vision of the desert, of the mountains, of the dust on the road, of the long marches. He forgets himself in the rhythmic swing of an old waltz, or in the quickstep of an ancient polka. They dance their national dances, their folk dances, in a cloud of smoke and dust. Drunk not only with the wine, but with all the songs and dances and stories, they forget themselves. . . . They forget their sorrows . . . their griefs . . . everything. . . .

When several battalions of the Legion are in town at the same time they dominate everything. They feel themselves free; nobody interferes with them. On their two pay days, the 1st and 15th of the month, they run everything. On those two days, guards on duty at the different posts in the town and camp are composed entirely of legionnaires. The patrols that are sent around the city after taps in the evening, to round up any delinquents, are always composed of legionnaires. All the other troops are kept in their barracks on those days in order to avoid trouble. A drunken legionnaire, or one who

49

is late in getting back to his barracks, if taken by a patrol of legionnaires will go along with them quietly, but if taken by a patrol of other troops, trouble will start at once. Considering himself on a higher plane than the others, he feels himself insulted if reprimanded or taken into custody by men of units other than the Legion.

But the legionnaire soon gets tired of life in garrison in the barracks. He likes to live under a tent, to be in the open air, to wash himself in a creek running near the camp. He likes movement, action, open places, and the road. The mountains and the desert become his sphere. It is there he expands and feels himself to be at his best.

Every quarter year we have to present legionnaires to be advanced in rank, to propose them to go to preparatory schools to become corporals and then sergeants.

A few of them refuse to be promoted, because they do not want responsibility. They say, "That is why we came here. It was to escape—not to have responsibility. Because we cannot think for ourselves we want others to think for us. That is why we are here. We submit to the discipline of the Legion, but we cannot ourselves discipline others."

One man, a tall, blond Dane, who spoke French

and English fluently and who came of very good family, was working as a secretary in the bureau of the battalion. I wanted him to be promoted, but he refused. I often asked him why he was there. His manner was cultivated, but there was a sadness in the expression of his eyes and face. He bore traces of suffering and great fatigue. Who was he? What was the matter with him? Had he committed some crime? I put him on the list of men that I wanted to promote, but he came to see me. He had a beautiful voice, so agreeable and appealing. He said:

"I thank you very much that you thought me worthy to be proposed for a corporal, but, please, leave me as a simple legionnaire. I am weak, and I cannot assume responsibility, and you will be the first to regret it if you give me any rank."

And, as if to prove his doubt of himself, a few weeks afterwards he began to drink heavily, and I was obliged to send him away from the bureau and put him in the ranks.

Among the recruits that arrived in Tadla were two youngsters of nineteen and twenty. They called themselves brothers. Were they really brothers? No one knew. In their military book, under nationality, there was written "Saloniki."

I said to them once, "It is all right, but there is no such nation as Saloniki. Are you Greeks?"

"No," they answered.

"Turks?"

"No."

"Are you Macedonians? Serbians? Dalmatians? Bulgars?"

The reply was always, "No. No. No." They were just Salonikis. That was all the answer I could get. When the sergeant major presented some papers for me to sign, among them was a report on the nationalities of the men in the unit. Against the names of the two Salonikis he had written "*Divers*" (miscellaneous).

V

WE PENETRATE THE ATLAS MOUNTAINS

KASBAH TADLA
April 29, 1923

THE 1st of May a *groupe mobile* is leaving Kasbah Tadla to undertake other operations.

For some time a large detachment of our forces was concentrated in Tadla. Friendly native troops from all the region were gathering around the camp on the outskirts of the town. An expedition was being prepared—one of the most important of the season. Many of the mountain tribes that were a menace to their neighbors had to be subdued. Some were already negotiating conditions upon which they would open their country to us, and would submit themselves to the general rule of the Moroccan Sultan. These mountain tribes believed in the right and the might of the strongest, and a display of arms had to be shown to them. We had to demonstrate that the Sultan of Morocco is protected by a powerful nation.

The Legion had to play its part in this advance, that would open this rich and prosperous country for the greater good of all.

After that is finished my unit is to take garrison in several outposts in the mountains. To be confined in some remote post with no possibility of going outside of four walls is not very thrilling, but one has to take his turn when it comes. Yet it is with a certain pleasure that I shall see my men and myself installed for three months in the fortifications, to live there quietly after a month of campaigning. I am getting books for my men in order that they may read in their leisure hours.

OUED ZEMKIL
May 2nd

The first day of our march we went only five miles, and we camped alongside the river. We left Kasbah Tadla purposely one day ahead in order to rest in the field for a day, and prepare our men physically and morally for the march and their hard task. They received their pay, and then all the next day they went from one café to another, and on the day of departure they were completely dazed and weakened. Even the five miles that we made, they covered with great difficulty. But a day of rest gave them strength.

54

May 3rd

The country we are going through is very rich. We have walked for more than four hours on a trail that goes through a cultivated plain with wonderful pastures. Hundreds of heads of cattle graze on these plains.

We went through prosperous native villages, and in the evening we reached the hills in the vicinity of the outpost of Taghzirt. We were facing a high mountain that we will have to climb soon in order to reach the crest and build another outpost. There we shall place our artillery to command all this fertile region.

Yesterday the sun was very hot. The heat has made all the men nervous, and one has to use all his patience in order to remain good-humored.

It is possible that before the beginning of the operation, many of the chieftains of the unsubdued tribes will come and ask us to treat with them, and that everything will be ended in a peaceful manner. It is also possible that when we march on their villages, they will run away and hide in the mountains, or that they will fire upon us from here and there. But within a short time they are certain to come back, when they see that we mean no harm. And in a few years they will become the same peaceful peas-

55

ants as other tribes, who before our arrival were also fierce fighters.

We are camping near the Drent river, narrow but deep that comes down rapidly from the mountain. From my tent I hear the sound of the flowing gray waters. . . .

OUED DRENT
May 6th

We occupy now the mountain of Bou Mahdi which dominates this region. One battalion of the Legion which held it before us remained there isolated for two days without water. An outpost must be built there. We had to put thousands of men to work to make a trail for the mules to carry water to the battalion. For two days we worked from four o'clock in the morning until eight o'clock in the evening.

The heat is very trying and no one can sleep. The sirocco continues to blow, and there is a humidity which enervates every one. It is difficult to manage the men. One has to suppress in oneself all signs of irritation and exert great self-control in order to go on with the day's work.

This life with the troops is a valuable school for any man, and especially for the young officers who come here for the first time. The torrid heat beats down on the plain, and one feels shriveled by it. The tense, blue sky seems to send down waves of liquid flame, that penetrate into you and hinder your respiration. Only from time to time the breeze coming from the tops of the mountains brightens your spirit.

ANOUFI TAHANSALT
May 9th

Numerous gatherings of mountain tribes are reported near Anoufi. Many groups of them are camping south of the town. We have also received information that a native religious chief is inciting the people who inhabit the rich valleys to resist our advance, and because of all this, the affair of Anoufi promises to be very lively and interesting.

From mouth to mouth news is spreading with great rapidity all over Morocco.

During the winter preceding our arrival strange men came telling the natives tales of warfare carried on far away in northern Morocco. On many occasions these men distributed money to the local *Marabouts* or saints living in monasteries. They tried to incite the tribes to rise against the Sultan of Morocco, who had long been under the protection of the French. They related that another Sultan, much more powerful, would soon come. He had already inflicted great losses on one European country,

57

Spain, and soon he would come to conquer the French.

It is easy to start trouble here. The natives are most credulous, and rumors of conflict excite them. Their ambition and pride can be nourished only by battle and warfare.

A merchant, a young, tall and slender Berber, came into my tent to-day. He offered to sell potatoes, cabbage and newly laid eggs. We agreed as to quantity and price and the deal seemed concluded. But he still stayed, and seeing him hesitate to go away, I suspected that he had something to say that had nothing to do with potatoes and cabbages.

"Speak to me, Ali," I encouraged him. "Is there something else?"

"I am so unworthy to speak to the hakem," he said. "Allah be praised! Who am I to reveal to you what you must know already?" He was silent for a moment. Then coming very close to me he whispered in my ear:

"Go, go quickly into the mountains, advance swiftly, there is no time to lose. Move along with all the forces you have and assure the population that you are strong and powerful. Roumis are beaten in the north. A whole Spanish armada is conquered by a man called Abd el Krim. He is as

58

cunning as a fox and strong as a tiger. He has the blessing of Allah—and he has cases of gold given to him by white men. . . . Remember, Ali, the unworthy servant of Allah, tells you this."

He bowed and disappeared. Not long after we were to learn that this native merchant spoke the truth.

According to the disposition of the maneuver, I had to march with the advance guard. On my right there was a company of Moroccan sharpshooters, and on my left flank, a company of our own regiment. The advance guard was very picturesque. It was composed of friendly natives, who had come from far-away regions, led by their local chiefs. On their small Arab horses they could easily outstrip us. They would dash ahead, and we would see them racing up the mountains or galloping rapidly through the valleys, standing high in their saddles and firing their rifles into the air.

Contrary to our expectation of resistance, there was none whatsoever, and when the friendly natives and our cavalry had topped the mountains, the inhabitants assembled to greet us. They asked that no harm be done to them and that we should not trample down their sown fields. But while these natives negotiated with us, on our left quick rifle fire was heard, and immediately my unit received an order to ocupy the heights from which this shooting came. Following us was the artillery that had to be installed on the positions we were instructed to occupy. We were obliged to go through a valley more than a mile and a half long. We were fired upon from the hills. But the legionnaires always steadily quicken their march when they are approaching their objective. With bayonets drawn, they rushed up the slope, and occupied it without firing a shot. I signalled immediately:

"Objective reached. No losses."

I received this reply:

"Bravo la Legion. Felicitations!"

When we reached the crest, we could see several villages with their fortified houses, their kasbahs, their fenced gardens. After an hour's stop, the movement forward began again. We had to ocupy Anoufi before dark.

Again the friendly natives went ahead to protect our flanks, and again the Legion had the honor of attack. Encouraged by the success of the morning, the men were eager to advance. They waited only for the bugle to order them to start. Precise orders were given to each section and to every company of the battalion, and everybody knew exactly his objective.

Among the rocks were large and deep grottoes

from which groups of hostile natives were fighting. Every small unit in our command had its grotto to occupy, and when finally the order to march came, everybody knew what he had to do. There was no confusion. There was no hesitation. And the natives, not expecting such a bold rush, and such a swift mastery of ground on the part of the white troops, were overcome with surprise and threw down their arms before the bayonets of the Legionnaires reached them.

By two o'clock in the afternoon we were masters of the situation. The troops were on a dominating plateau, but the day's work was not ended. We had to fortify our camp, and while this was being done by part of the troops, another part had to bring all the wounded from the field to the hospital tents that were pitched immediately in the middle of the camp. Other units had to help make the road passable for the artillery. The troops had had nothing to eat that day, and food had to be prepared. Still others were detailed to bring in water from a spring that ran below the camp, and to start a fire. In less than an hour after we reached camp all this work was progressing in the manner peculiar to troops in campaign. Not until seven o'clock in the evening was the work finished and the men free to rest.

Among the men were four musicians. They composed the orchestra of the battalion. At my first luncheon in the officers' mess, one of them, a Prussian named Bohlman, attracted my attention. He was very tall, thin, with a small, well-shaped head on a fine neck—his head all shaved as Prussian officers' heads always are.

He played the violin. Even when playing gay dances his instrument always had a note of sadness in it. His face wore an expression of extreme tenseness and suffering. And his eyes, gray, with almost no expression, cold, void of all sentiment, were not in accord with his features. It seemed as if all life had been taken from them. I said to an officer near me, "That man will commit suicide sometime."

A few months later the battalion was on the road. Heat and dust! The men tired, almost exhausted, but going on always, still farther, helped by a song that would stir them up, or by some joke that would enliven them. I noticed the musician. He was taller than the rest, but short of wind. I had noticed him before—he could not keep pace with the others. Yet he never asked to be relieved from his heavy pack, or to be put in the wagons if there were any. He would get to camp perhaps half an hour later than the others, when darkness was already fall-

62

ing. But he would come. Once when I saw him arrive exhausted, I told him that I would make him a driver of one of the wagons, because I knew that it was hard for him to walk.

Pulling himself together and standing at perfect attention, he said: "No, sir, I am an ex-officer. I will endure the hardships of a soldier, but never the easy job of a driver."

Then to-day when we had reached a stopping place, the sergeant came to me and said, "Bohlman has killed himself."

I went to see the body of the musician. I asked who had been near him at the time. A man who also could not keep pace, said, "I was near him. Bohlman stopped. I went ahead. Then I heard the sound of something. Turning, I saw Bohlman, bending forward, piercing his body with his bayonet, and at the same time he pulled the trigger. Then he fell to the ground."

May 12th

Immediately after occupying this region, which marks a new step of penetration into the mountains of Morocco, a group of outposts had to be constructed. The day after our arrival an appropriate place dominating the surrounding country was chosen for the principal outpost. The men of the

Foreign Legion are the ones who always construct these outposts.

After a few years we shall go farther. But these outposts will remain in the rear. They will be dismantled. They will serve then as shelter for passing caravans. Around them market places will be established, and the people will even forget that there was a time when the towers carried guns.

Only the cemeteries will record the struggles that took place there. These dismantled posts and cemeteries mark the steps of our advance. The means of the men who have fallen there will never be known, and indifferent people will not grant them any glory for their deeds. But they did not ask for recognition or for glory. Who could give them more than that which they felt in their own hearts, while doing the thing they believed to be right?

Life with the legionnaires is intense. Weak men perish as a fruit blossom touched by the frost. When one sees the fortified camps, the roads, the bridges that span deep gorges—all constructed by these men during the operations—one has the greatest admiration for their magnificent endurance. Here man feels himself inspired. He goes beyond himself. His strength is tested every hour, and the harder he

64

works the more he has courage to continue, and the more confidence he has in himself.

Blond men of all races, French, Slav, German, Anglo-Saxon, Scandinavian, are able to resist the heat and suffering here, while colored men fall by the wayside exhausted.

When the natives see our men bareheaded with torso nude, working steadily throughout the day under the burning African sun, they feel that they are in the presence of a superior race.

Some of the Berber tribes are still savage. They are most audacious. At night, absolutely naked, with knives in their teeth, they slip through the barbed wire into the camp and try to cut the throat of the sentry, and take away his rifle.

The other night, one Berber came into the middle of the camp, about ten yards from the tents of the officers. He even entered the tent of the orderlies, and got two rifles. Discovered and chased, he succeeded in getting away. Almost every day they attack the convoys, and no one risks going out of the camp without an escort.

May 18th

It is hard even to describe the beauty of an early morning bathed in sunshine, with the snow peaks of the Atlas Mountains all rose color from the reflection of the morning sun. It is wonderful to feel the joy of existence, and the surrounding beauty. One feels like chanting and dancing. Many times during the day one lifts one's eyes to the sun, and is almost suffocated with emotion.

May 24th

All the operations in this region were concluded without great loss of life. Some of the men, who ventured too far away from the camp, were assassinated by brigands roaming around in search of loot. A sentry at night was sometimes stopped, and his rifle taken away. A convoy not sufficiently guarded was attacked in a mountain pass.

To-day, very near to our camp, a human body was found, a soldier of the Legion, Russian by birth. Who killed him no one knows, but since all his clothes were taken it is certain that he was attacked by natives.

There has been little actual fighting. The natives watch closely everything we do. They size up our strength. They see that we are building our outposts—that we intend to remain here. They weigh the outcome in their minds—what advantage it will be to them. How will they benefit by it?

All the troops that had to come to this region are now being withdrawn. The only soldiers that remain

66

are the garrisons of the outposts that have just been constructed. Under cover of these armed outposts, new life will begin. Those who need protection will find it, and those who disturb the general peace that is to prevail from now on in this country will be punished.

VI

GARDENS AND GRAVE-
STONES

WE left the Territory of Tadla and started off
for the region of Marrakech. There on the
banks of the river *Oued el Abid* I shall be in charge
of the Ouaouizeght group of outposts built two years
ago.

This line of outposts protects the new road that
we recently constructed connecting Tadla and Marrakech via Azilal. This new road opened for us one
of the richest districts in Morocco, which before our
arrival lay in waste.

We are traversing an interesting region, very
uneven and mountainous. Wonderful kasbahs, built
very high of red earth, have shown us their thick
walls and high towers. Superb gardens are around
these kasbahs—almond trees, figs, pomegranates,
and groves of olive trees. We crossed the ridge of
the mountain and arrived on the southern slope of
the Middle Atlas.

68

My heart sank when, from afar, I saw the post of Ouaouizeght where I am to remain for the next five months, completely isolated from the rest of the world. I shall be alone with less than half my men, with all my officers detached to other posts of this group.

There is an outpost not far away where an officer and thirty men have to remain. It is built on a very high peak and has no water. Water must be carried there every eight days on mules. One can imagine the life of a young officer under these conditions. A noncommissioned officer and fifteen men are detached to a blockhouse still higher in the mountain.

Tizi R'Nim
June 4th

On our way here we passed near a few outposts in the mountains occupied by the Legion. The men on the outlook would signal our approach. The bugler of Tizi R'Nim sent a greeting to us—an air indicating the number of his regiment and of his battalion . . . and then the refrain of the "March of the Legion." Our bugler replied with the same refrain, and indicated our unit. These sounds of the bugle, in the midst of the African mountains, made us feel that we were not alone, that our men were everywhere, vigilant friends at the outposts of civilization.

June 5th

The relief of an outpost is always a solemn affair.
The men to be relieved, in full campaign dress, are
standing in line on either side of the gates outside
of the post. At the sound of the bugle, while they
present arms, we march through these lines into the
courtyard and camp there temporarily. While the
officers are busy handing over orders and an inven-
tory of all materials, arms and foodstuffs to the
new commander, the legionnaires fraternize with one
another. A meal is always prepared for those who
arrive. Noncommissioned officers are designated to
replace those who are relieved. Telephone operators
are exchanged. Everything changes hands.

OUAOUIZEGHT
June 6th

The first night we are the guests of the old garrison, and no duties are performed. But in the morning we take charge and are responsible for the security of everything and everybody.

Some of my men are starting in the early morning
to go to farther outposts, to relieve them also. The
distances between these posts are not great. In the
evening the replaced men gather at the central post.

On these occasions the buglers have much to do—
70

they salute those who come, and they sound "good-by" to the outgoing troops. During the whole day there is much noise with all this coming and going.

Early in the morning those who are to remain assemble outside the post. And between the two lines of legionnaires presenting arms to their comrades, the outgoing troops pass through and start away. The buglers continue with their calls. The sounds echo in the mountains and fill this clear transparent air, and from mountain to mountain the refrain of the Legion resounds—the refrain of comradeship, of common work in the spirit of the great brotherhood of man.

Then silence falls. All is quiet, peaceful. The excitement of the two days is past. The men in the outpost remain alone. They are quiet. They are lonely. And they fill the first night with their sad songs. In the morning life begins anew.

June 10th

I remain with about sixty men and my administrative bureau. The commander of a post has many things to do. He has a thousand duties—he is commander of the post, commander of his unit, manager of the commissariat and of the supply of armaments for the entire region. All the troops in this section of the country are supplied by me. I am a grocer, a

71

bread baker (we have two ovens to make bread for the troops in this region), and a butcher. Not only must meat be furnished, but I also have to make contracts and buy the live stock. I have to deliver sugar, flour, lard, wine, and oats and hay for the animals. Construction material must be delivered also.

An officer has to furnish many reports to different bureaus. He is responsible not only for the discipline, but also for all the material and foodstuffs deposited in his post.

Already there are small annoyances. The guard of the general store, a good type of Russian, reported to me that his chief, a corporal, whom I had put in charge of the foodstuffs, had admitted some irregularities in his conduct. He had drunk wine belonging to the administration; he had given out bread without writing down in the books the amount of money he received. After making inquiry, I found that this had really happened. I put the man in prison and appointed another who will be more honest.

Each day is full, and one does not have a moment to oneself. Everybody comes to the commanding officer with every little thing. The nights are not very calm, either. There are brigands around the post. In these first days, when the men of every rank are unfamiliar with the place, everything has to be organized and shaped.

July 15th

Since we came here much work has been done. We have planted a vegetable garden near the post, and although the men were skeptical about planting in June, it has come out wonderfully. One of my gardeners is a Swiss, who knows how to do the planting. Another man was very ingenious in capturing a stream flowing not far away and making a complete system of irrigation. At daybreak, when the gates of the post are thrown open, the two men, the gardener and the irrigator, go out and water the garden. In the evening, after the day's work is done and the evening meal eaten, there remain about two or three hours of leisure before the men go to bed, and there is always a procession of them going out to see the garden. One sees groups of legionnaires of different nationalities stopping at one corner or another of it, discussing the plants, and talking about gardens and plants in their own countries.

There is such a tender expression on the faces of men who watch a growing plant—something that comes out of the earth, something that is brought forth by the will and energy of men, something that is created. The transmutation of matter. . . . The creation of new forms. . . . What mystery!

July 21st

Very soon two more stone barracks will be ready. We have built them since we came here. The other outposts, the smaller ones that are in our group, have also been enlarged by new buildings, and the old ones have been repaired.

Lime is needed for whitening the walls, and two of my outposts have chosen a suitable place between their walls and the barbed wire to excavate and build a lime-kiln. In the vicinity we have found gypsum and have made plaster with which to whiten the walls of our rooms. In addition to this Sergeant Montana, an Italian, has told me that he has found marble not far away.

One day Montana went out in charge of a gang of men who were bringing stone from a quarry we had established in the vicinity. While looking over the ground he discovered the marble—white with rose veins. He came to me in the evening, at sunset, with several pieces in his hand. He is an old soldier—a legionnaire before the Great War. He served all through it. He was wounded many times, and many times decorated. After the war he came back to Algeria, and then went to Morocco with his battalion. He is small, round-shouldered—almost a hunchback. His short legs are bowed, and when he walks they almost form a circle. He is built of good material, though—only the carpentry is bad. No work, no march, could ever tire him. Patient, almost phlegmatic, with impassive eyes, he is a steady and most reliable man, and one from whom advice could be taken on account of his experience.

He stood there before me.

"There is plenty of it," he said. "What shall we do with it? How shall we use it?"

I saw that he had an idea of his own. After a moment's silence he went on:

"If you will allow me, I should like to bring some of the big pieces into the post. Why not make crosses for our dead? I can cut the crosses out of the marble, and on them I can engrave the names."

He gave the word "dead" a warmth of tone that touched me. . . . It was decided that he was to bring in the marble. After that I would see him with his chisel and hammer cutting out the crosses—one . . . two . . . three . . . four . . . five . . . and   on them he engraved the names—Lefort . . . Blukher . . . Theodoroff . . . Schultz . . Lopez . . . Konenko . . . Arkadieff . . . Johnson . . . many . . . many. . . . Their age also he engraved on the cross, and the date of their entrance into the Legion and the date of their departure.

One after another the crosses were set into the ground.

At sunset he would go to the cemetery accompanied by a few of the men. There they would tend the graves, and then, silent they lingered there, one . . . two . . . three minutes or more. God alone knew their thoughts. They returned to the post just before the bugle sounded retreat.

July 25th

We made our own brick. The clay soil was suitable for it. First we dug holes in the ground. In them we put water, straw and clay. Afterward this mass would be shaped and dried in the sun. It furnished good material for construction. The days were hot. The men, almost naked, would take turns standing in the holes and mixing the mud with their bare feet. Hard work, but what a satisfaction for them to see more than seven hundred bricks made in one day. "We have done what the others could not do," they would say.

There is always much more enthusiasm among men when they work for the common good than when they work only for themselves.

Two of the corporals—one an Austrian, a former
76

opera singer, and the other a Russian, a student of technology—had proved themselves to be excellent masons. One day they asked me if they could build a new house for the commander of the post. The student of technology brought me a plan of the house— he had drawn it himself—a simple one with two rooms, and at either side of the door there was a column supporting the gable roof. They asked to be exempted from duty for two weeks, and promised to finish the job within that time.

Never, never in my life have I seen men work with such joy and forgetfulness. They were on their job from dawn to sunset, singing all day long. These two corporals, with the aid of two other men, whom they were allowed to choose, did all the work. They carried all the material themselves. They made their own lime. They plastered the walls. They made a roof of branches over which they laid earth, then more branches, and finally they covered it all with sheets of tin.

They even made cement floors. I wondered where the cement came from. It was not in the post. I asked them. "We managed to get it," was all they would say. The fact was that when a convoy was going to the rear, they gave instructions to the mule-teers to steal sacks of cement from the commissariat department.

Every morning after the sun has risen, the night guard has to be replaced by the day watch. The day watch is assembled in the courtyard of the post; lined up in single file they stand there awaiting the command. The sergeant of the guard comes up to the bugler, who is standing a few yards in front of the assembled guard, waiting also for orders.

The sergeant commands *Garde à vous!* Arms are presented. *Au drapeau!* And the flag is being raised over the post, slowly rising above the white walls, and taken by the morning wind into the blue sky. Every man who is outside of the barracks in the post, even all the natives who are living in the annex, when they hear the bugle and see the flag rising, stop and stand motionless. Perfect silence reigns.

There is another moment of emotion at the lowering of the flag in the evening, when the day watch is replaced by the night guard. The night guard assembles facing the flag, the bugler again blows *Garde à vous!* and the flag is lowered for the night.

July 30th

There are no distractions in the outpost. One is confined to its four walls. But outside the post, built against its wall, there are three canteens. The men go there on the days after they receive their pay and they spend all their money. For about two days every fortnight almost everybody is drunk, and one has to have untiring energy in order to control these men, who come from all corners of the earth.

An outpost has a life of its own. And it is needful that this life should be organized according to the needs of the men and the service that they are to perform. Special attention must be paid to their food, and their rights must be respected. Every man receives a quart of wine each day and one has to see that this liquid is never lacking in the post. It is the same with bread. It must be always fresh and baked well. Otherwise the men grumble; and no effective work can be demanded of men when they think they have been deprived of their rights.

These days I have three shifts making bread, because there are several units in the vicinity that are engaged in road construction.

Very soon another campaign which will take us still farther into the mountains will be started. Already a base for the future operations has been installed not far from here, and all the men at that base are also supplied with food by my post.

VII

TYPES OF LEGIONNAIRES

Ouaouizeght
August 10, 1923

WHEN I first came here I was told that my
post would become a center of future ex-
pansion in this region, and therefore I immediately
undertook the enlargement of Ouaouizeght. Now we
are quite ready. I have even built a barrack thirty
yards long for a depot for foodstuffs. In September
food supplies to last nine months will be stored here,
and if the roads during the winter become impassable, on account of the rain, the men of the outposts
in this region and the natives, who depend on us for
many things, will want for nothing. Yes, everything
is ready, and I am waiting only for the doors and
windows to come and be put in the new buildings.

August 12th

To-day a general and twelve officers came to visit
my post and the outposts under my command, in
order to observe the country and to have a full view
80

of the far-away mountains where we shall go next. They were well received on a small terrace that I had put up alongside the wall, under the branches of a giant olive tree, which is one of four trees being left inside the post. A long table was dressed by my orderly, and on it flowers had been placed in empty shells carved by the men.

The general reviewed the men. Unfortunately, his visit coincided with payday and many of them were drunk. Yet they all kept up their appearance and stood erect and solemnly smart. After the superior officer went away the post returned to its usual life.

August 15th

To-day a man who was drunk became a nuisance to everybody. He was locked up. His friend, also drunk, came to my lodging and asked that he be released. The petitioner was a Frenchman from Brest, who had enlisted in the Legion as a Belgian. An ex-marine, he had been for a long time in a military prison for discipline. This man was not young. He was about fifty, very tall, and still strong. When he came to my lodgings and asked that his friend be liberated, I told him that I was surprised to see such an old soldier so lacking in discipline; because no one is allowed to come directly to me and make a

81

request at a time which is not the regular hour when I see men presented by the sergeant major.

He was in a rather talkative mood. First he began to excuse himself and then he went on to tell of his miserable life, relating family misfortunes, and gradually opening his heart to me.

I always dreaded confessions of the legionnaires, because these confessions were usually made when the men were not accountable for their actions, and almost always they regret a confession made to a commanding officer.

Several times I wanted to stop this legionnaire from talking, from saying things that he would regret afterwards, but his desire to talk was too strong. He just went on and on telling me things, and in the glitter of his eye I saw a certain hatred toward me. But he could not stop. When he walked out of my room I was disturbed and I asked myself, What will he do next? as I knew him to be a very undisciplined man, ready always for all kinds of wild actions.

When darkness fell upon the outpost, I stepped out of my lodging and went to visit the towers upon which the sentries stood, guarding the outpost. I came to the first tower, which was near the entrance of the post, and, quietly approaching the sentry, I saw that near him was the figure of a man. Coming still nearer I saw the man bend toward the sentry and

82

give him his water bottle, and the sentry drank. I reached for the water bottle and smelled it. It was wine. I spilled the wine on the ground. The man was the French legionnaire who an hour ago had walked out of my rooms.

I said, "What are you doing here, Latour? Is that your water bottle?"

"Yes, it is mine," he replied.

"What are you doing here?" I repeated.

He said, "I am in the group of sentries and I am to relieve this sentry when his time expires."

I told him to go to his place and leave the sentry alone. Then I went back to my lodging. I was worried. There were two candles burning on my table. The door of the lodging was open and from these candles came the only light that streamed through the doorway into the darkness of the court-yard.

I went out again. Turning to the right I heard the click of a gun. I stopped. I was not in the path of the light. I was in the shadow and I could see a man coming toward my lodging with his rifle cocked. As he came nearer I recognized Latour. I saw him clearly in the candlelight issuing from my room. When he was within a few yards of my door I stepped out of the darkness and was close to him. He stopped and discharged his rifle, and I heard the bullet strike the ground. Looking straight into his face I said:

"What do you want, Latour? Why are you here?"

"Latour is taking a walk."

I said, *"Bonne promenade."*

Then I whistled. My orderly came, and then the sergeant in charge of the guard. I told the sergeant to take Latour away, disarm him, and put him under guard. Then I also ordered him to change the group of sentries of Tower No. 1.

Latour had had twelve years of service, and if I were to report on his action of that night, he would be court-martialed and perhaps sentenced to from three to ten years in prison. I did not want to do it. I only gave him the maximum punishment that we can give to legionnaires without referring the case to the court. I gave as a reason for his punishment:

"Legionnaire Latour, being in a group of sentries, left his place; gave intoxicating drink to another sentry; and afterwards, with his rifle loaded, he was found in the vicinity of the lodging of his commander and he could not explain his presence there."

In the morning I called him. I read him his sentence. He stood erect and avoided looking at my eyes. The same day I relieved twelve men from a very far-away blockhouse in my group, and I sent Latour there. Several times I visited this block-house, and as I would approach the sergeant who commanded it would call out his men. Latour was there, always standing in the most perfect manner, presenting arms. I would ask him:

"*Ça va, Latour?*"

He would always reply, "*Ça va . . . content. . . .*"

August 17th

A detachment of new men has arrived at the post. One after another they were presented to me in my lodging. One broad-shouldered fellow entered, saluted and then took off his hat. I saw on his fore-head, tattooed in large letters, this word, "*Fatalité.*" I shivered when I saw it. His name sounded French. I asked him whether he was French. He said no, he was Belgian. Looking at his records I saw that he had just come from serving two years in a military prison. I told him that I would not judge him by his past, but by his future behavior. He said that he would do his best, but that he was not sure of himself. Not wanting to go into details, I dismissed him. A week later, when the company had assembled to go to work, he flatly refused to obey orders. The adjutant came to me and reported it.

I asked, "What reasons does the man give?"

He said, "He gave me no reasons. He just refused to go."

I told the adjutant to read to him the article of law that relates to infractions of that kind.

"Oh, but when I started to read it to him, he repeated to me the entire article, and said he was quite aware of what he was doing. He simply refused."

I asked that the man be brought before me. He came. He saluted. He looked straight into my face.

I said, "What is the matter?"

He replied, "Yes, I know what I am doing. I refuse. And for it I will get from three to five years more. I don't mind."

I wanted to talk to him, but he stopped me.

"No, please. No use. I know all you are going to say. No moral teaching for me. I know. My worst enemy is myself. But that's how I was born. I owe it to my parents."

He saluted and walked out.

August 20th

Once, talking with a sergeant about the men in his section, he said to me:

"I have a terrible man in my section. He isn't bad, and yet nobody knows what he will do next."

86

I said, "Who is it?"

He replied, "Le Fourne."

"But no. I know Le Fourne. I like him. I think he is wonderful. This man is always the first to wake up in the morning, no matter what the weather or how tired he may be after a long march, to prepare for the men something hot to eat or to drink, to start a fire under the most unfavorable and terrible conditions, in rain or snow or dampness. And he always carries, beside his heavy pack, pieces of wood to kindle a fire. And I have seen him doing that for months and months."

The sergeant asked, "Do you know his record?"

"Yes. There is nothing in his book."

"It isn't from his book that I know. His book says nothing. He enlisted under a false name and nationality. Three times during the Great War he was condemned. The first time he was sentenced to ten years in prison, the second time to twelve years and the third time to eight years—each time for desertion. He always escaped from the prison. Captured again, he would be convicted once more— then another escape—another conviction. I don't know that he ever served more than three years in prison, although sentenced to more than thirty years. Finally he escaped once more, and here he is in the Legion."

I asked him if he was sure of these facts.

"Yes," he said. "Le Fourne told them to me himself."

I began to watch Le Fourne closely, but I could find nothing that would indicate his former misbehavior. He was always the same placid quiet man, going on with his daily tasks as regularly as any of the others, and perhaps better than some.

And then after a campaign, came the quiet life, the confined life of the post. He was made head cook. The men liked the way he prepared their food. He was clean himself and he kept everything in perfect order. But, after a month of this stable life, I noticed that the quiet expression on his face was changing. There was something stirring in him. He was restless and uneasy. Sometimes I would walk in upon him unannounced. I would find him lying on his cot, with his hands under his head, and with a strange look in his eyes. Seeing me he would jump from his bed and stand at attention. I would ask him, "What is it, Le Fourne? What is the matter with you? Do you need some help? Have you received bad news? Something wrong?"

He would shake his head to every question of mine. No . . . no . . . no . . . there was nothing the matter. As to news—he received no news . . . never received any news. He had no one to write to him.

88

Then I would say, "Is there something the matter with you? You want to be relieved perhaps from this job? You are tired of it?"

"No . . . no . . . . I am content. There's nothing wrong with me."

But yet I saw that some deep, troubled thoughts were undermining him.

Finally the climax came. I was sitting alone on my terrace. My orderly was looking out at the blue-veiled hills and mountains far away, saying how beautiful they were. I heard a sound from the other courtyard, and hurried steps approaching. A sergeant, pale and frightened, came up.

"It is Le Fourne," he gasped.

Within a minute I saw Le Fourne, his hair in disorder, with blood on his mouth, his eyes absolutely mad, his garments torn, led by two sergeants, coming toward me. I asked the sergeants to leave him alone with me.

"No, please hold me. I beg of you, commander, let them hold me, for I am not responsible." And then he added, "Well, it is all over. Back to prison."

What had happened was this: the kitchen was next to the mess of the noncommissioned officers. About twelve of them were finishing their luncheon and chatting around a bottle of wine when Le Fourne appeared with a long kitchen knife in his hand. He stood in the door and said: "Ah, now I have got you! I will stab every one of you now! I hate you all!" And he rushed at the nearest man. But everybody jumped on him. Several were wounded slightly in attempting to take away the knife. Then he was overpowered.

He was led to the prison door by two men with bayonets fixed. When the door was opened, before entering the prison, he wheeled around and with his right foot kicked the chest of the sergeant, who fell unconscious.

Next day I went to see Le Fourne. The prison door was opened and the legionnaire appeared before me. I told the guard to leave us alone. We stood there before each other, and neither one of us spoke a word. We were both moved by the meeting. After a long pause I saw my man tremble and then fall on his knees. Covering his face with both hands he wept like a child. I lifted him up and took his hands from his face. There was a childlike look in his eyes.

"Why have you done it?" I asked.

"I don't know. It gets me. If I were normal I would not be here perhaps. The world has done me great harm, and I could not fight the world. And I could not fight out in myself my bad character. I could not live by the rules laid down by society. I could not fight against the hatred that sometimes choked me and overwhelmed me. I came here to find forgetfulness in battle . . . in hardship . . . in work. Not being able to command my own life, I wanted to be commanded, always commanded in a harsh, rough way. My spirit of rebellion against everybody—everything—against life itself, had to be conquered by others. I had to be worked to death —and I was not.

"Here life was too quiet, too placid, too regular, and I had too much leisure and freedom. And then the poison that is within me came once more to the surface. The hate, I mean. I had to find an outlet, and I did what I did. I kicked the sergeant yesterday because then I had not gotten rid of all the hatred that was in me.

"Only when I did that did I feel it was gone. I knocked my head against the prison walls when I was alone. I cried all night. Now I am harmless. I have pity for myself, for others, and I am awaiting the hard labor they will sentence me to as a liberation from myself."

With his head down, Le Fourne turned toward the prison and walked in. He was sentenced to three years.

VIII

TO THE RESCUE OF
PEACEFUL TRIBES

Ouaouizeght
August 21, 1923

RUMORS of trouble in the mountains are increasing. We have information that the mountain tribes are restless; that they are holding meetings and that they are divided in opinion as to whether they will submit to the central rule of Morocco, or remain independent and continue their seminomadic life. A few of the big chiefs are advocating submission to the Sultan, but others are opposed to it. They are quarreling one with another. Many, I am told, have been killed. And, as a reflection of this uneasiness in the mountains, there is uneasiness also in the whole country. One has to be extremely careful. But fortunately the nights are not so black. It is the first quarter of the moon and from the bastions of the post one is able to see the country all around.

August 22nd

The south wind is blowing fiercely. Not a tree,

not a shrub, not even the grass can stand against this wind, which kills everything in its path. Men have to have good health and great endurance in order to stand this wind, which seems to come right from hell itself. Here in the post we are more or less sheltered. There is water near by, fresh water, of which one can drink as much as one likes. A few weeks ago the operations that had to be undertaken here began. . . . Large detachments of troops went out into the mountains. They are now in the open, living under tents, where water is scarce. They have to endure great hardships. Only one who has experienced a situation like this and all the privations connected with it is able to understand the terrible conditions under which our troops live here in the midst of summer. The operation that is going on in the mountains to the south of us is developing successfully, but, of course, not without loss of life. One man was buried to-day in the cemetery at our post. A young Frenchman.

There is something tragic in living near a cemetery. Little by little it is being populated. I assisted to-day when they dug the grave. This red earth thrown up by the shovel of a legionnaire opens itself to take back that which belongs to it. . . . The transmutation of matter. . .!

93

It seems to me that the soul does not leave the body for a few days, that it hovers around for some time. This evening, while taking a walk before the gates of the post were closed, I saw the most fantastic sunset of my life. The walls of the cemetery were red—and seemed to emit a kind of light that mingled with the rays of the setting sun—as though the spirits of those whose bodies are here were having difficulty in detaching themselves to begin another life.

August 23rd

An outpost is called upon to shelter strange visitors. To-day a caravan of camels passed in the vicinity, and fearing to be attacked by some armed wanderers at night, the chief of the caravan came and asked permission to bring all his animals under the shelter of the walls of the post. Forty—fifty—sixty camels slowly walked in. For the night they knelt down in rows facing each other, with a narrow pathway between. And a curious sensation comes over one who passes between them at nighttime—their strange faces, weaving their heads from side to side, chewing and sniffing the air. It seems to me that ostriches and camels resemble one another in their way of walking and in the shape of the neck and head.

94

August 26th

The mornings just before dawn are very beautiful. The stars are pure and magnificent, and what silence fills the whole atmosphere! The sentries are vigilant at their posts and a slight breeze caresses the figures of these rough men. The sigh and the murmur of the river which descends from the mountains, mingling with the wind and the silence, form a mysterious symphony. They are strange, these voices of the night.

August 28th

There are a few native villages near my outpost. The natives have cultivated all the country near by which is very rich and fertile. They have planted wonderful gardens, and the olive groves, that had been neglected for many years, have been restored. To protect their property from tribes which have not yet submitted to the Central Government a blockhouse has been built on a height overlooking the village, the garrison of which is composed of the natives themselves commanded by a Moroccan in the regular service of the French Protectorate.

A few days ago all the men in the garrison were called out to participate in an operation in the mountains and only the old men, the women and the children remained in the village. That night

95

brigands came from the mountains and drove away the cattle. They attacked the dwellings of the natives. They killed off many of the men, women and children.

All night we heard the fusillade, yet we did not know where it came from.

At sunrise, when everybody got up and the gates of the post were opened, we heard many cries and shouts and much lamentation. I sent out several armed squads to search in the vicinity to find out what had happened. These squads reported the situation in the village and they brought back with them a few children with arms twisted and broken, who were in a most pitiable state. Immediately I sent all the medical aid at hand.

Occasions like this prove that our presence is needed here, whatever sacrifices it may involve, in order to protect the natives, who, if we should leave the country, would continue endlessly their futile warfare among themselves.

Civilization is not only a privilege, it is a burden —an honorable burden for those who are conscious of the benefits that it brings. With distances abolished by means of transportation, with all the mechanical inventions of the last century, it is our duty to make all countries safe—safe for the new-comer and for the commerce that may be developed.

96

Also we must give to these undeveloped, far-away people, shut off from our civilization, the benefits of the knowledge that we have acquired during past centuries. Along with the material development, which sometimes is very sporadic from not having a general scheme and aim, there must be developed a sense of coördination, in order to bring together, for the benefit of humanity, all that has been invented by individuals in one country or another. Any invention, any material improvement in our life is not an end in itself, but a means to better life. And if it is really to better the general conditions of life, it must be organized and coördinated. European civilization has gone far beyond its geographical boundaries and, therefore, it is not confined to one continent . . . even to one race or another. It is general. It is human. And, therefore, it is the obligation of this civilization to make the whole world, as it draws closer and closer together, a place where the achievements of its great men can be of benefit to every country.

September 2nd

During the three months of our stay the walls of the post were whitened, new barracks were built for the men, and a stable was erected for the horses and mules.

Then one day . . . an unforgettable day . . . two palm trees were planted in our garden outside the outpost. The trees were by a creek in the ravine. There were long and elaborate discussions as to whether the palms could be transplanted safely. Many opinions were expressed, and when it was decided that the plan was feasible, a delegation waited on me to ask permission. The ceremony was to take place on a Sunday. All the men who were free from duty went to the creek with shovels and ropes. The ground was dug up very carefully, all the roots were freed, the trees were wrapped, and then lovingly and carefully, they were carried to the garden, where they were planted.

The old bugler was there looking on, eagerly watching the operation. He, who on all important and thrilling occasions would sound his bugle, was he not to be allowed to announce the rite of planting? With his eyes he silently asked permission and silently it was given. Go on with your bugle, Kurtz!

Then from that bugle came such thrilling sounds . . . such plaintive notes . . . such outbursts of joy . . . such a wonderful Annunciation, carried by the winds of the mountains to all the corners of the world.

When I leave this post the one who will come to

relieve me will come to a fortress all white and clean and greatly enlarged. The commander will have for himself a house of two rooms, which I have had built, large barracks full of light for his men, and the garden which we have planted.

IX

DIFFICULTIES AND DANGERS

KASBAH TADLA
September 10, 1923

AFTER being shut up in an outpost for a few months the legionnaires are back in Tadla, busily at work constructing new buildings, adding new quarters to the military camp of the city.

September 25th

The sunset is magnificent. The whole eastern sky is suffused with rose. On the horizon one sees the mountains that close the way to the desert. The sky is of such incredible purity that it makes your heart contract. This beauty penetrates you with a radiant force that causes your spirit to fly to inexplicable heights. The west is in flame and the sun itself is of molten gold, dropping in cascades on the other side of the horizon.

The mornings also are beautiful. The plain is covered with green grass, wet with dew. The sun

100

begins to come out of the mountains, as a prince in a fairy tale.

One sees the Arabs leaving their kasbahs to work on the land. The buglers, the fifers, the drummers, are going out in the field for exercise and soon martial sounds spread over the plain. On the trails one sees native men and women walking in a file to the markets of Kasbah Tadla, driving before them donkeys loaded with all kinds of produce. One sees the shepherds driving their flocks. One hears the sound of the motors of aeroplanes that are leaving the ground and lifting themselves up into the sky.

I like to gallop my horse in this morning air, so cool and clear. The odor of the newly plowed ground and of the fresh grass is intoxicating. One feels oneself a part of the mysterious forces of nature.

September 30th

I have just arrived from Boujad, a town about twenty miles away from Tadla. From all the region the Arabs and the Berbers came to a cattle fair, where prizes were offered for the finest cattle raised in the vicinity. Only a few years ago these expositions were started in order to encourage the natives to raise cattle and also aid them to become interested in each other. These people, who before our coming, did not often meet for peaceful purposes, are now

101

beginning to get together for the welfare of their country. The mountain tribes show traces of many different races that migrated from the east to the west, settling down in different epochs in some mountainous country, to remain there and to establish a character and a type of their own!

The gathering was extremely picturesque.

On a vast plateau several hundred native horsemen, with very old and very long rifles in their hands, pointing these weapons into the air, filed in one long line, awaiting the arrival of the commander of the region. When we were within about two hundred yards of the horsemen they all shouted and yelled and rushed toward us at the wildest gallop, shooting into the air. For a moment I thought they would run us down, but when about twenty yards away all these hundreds of horsemen stopped short and simultaneously fired a shot into the air.

Then, placing ourselves at one end of this line, we galloped in front of them to the other end, and went into the tents that had been prepared for us. Under this brilliant and hot sun, in the extreme luminosity of the African noon, the horses with saddles and ornaments of chiseled iron and steel, gold and silver, with blankets thrown over them of blue, and red, and yellow and green, and gold, made an

102

extraordinarily vivid display. These men, old and young, were dressed in burnouses of different colors. The old men had long beards, the young ones a fringe of hair around their faces.

The tents had been placed on the top of a hill from which we could see the whole plain, where a horse race was to take place. The tents were rich with tapestries and carpets, and hundreds of cushions had been thrown on the ground. There were musicians in every tent, and when the race was finished, dancers came in, and every chief presented his own dancers to the assembled guests.

What a magnificent feast it was!

October 5th

To-day a small man, pale-faced, with a long, black beard, appeared before me. I asked him what he wanted—why he had asked to see me. Speaking rather good French in a deep, low voice, and bowing to me in a nonmilitary way, he said:

"Please, I want to be relieved from the place that I occupy now. A year ago I was made the guardian of the store here. All my comrades have gone to fight. They have endured great hardships. They have suffered from rain, and cold and heat, and I . . . I always remain comfortable in the store, quiet, undisturbed, leading an easy life. Please relieve me

103

from this post. I want to do the same service as the other men."

I told him that if he had been put in as guardian of the store it meant that the commanding officer had faith in him, that each one had his own place, and that he rendered good service to the whole unit by assuring the security of the store.

"Yes," he replied, "it is true, of course. But I cannot do it any more, because it is too easy for me. I came here to suffer. I came here to undergo great hardships . . . to try myself out. Please relieve me of this post. And then I must tell you another thing. I am too much alone, and I am afraid. I have been knocked down by life, and sometimes I lose control of myself, and I cannot answer for my actions."

I told him that I would see what I could do, and I questioned the corporal in charge of the store, who also slept there.

"What kind of a man is Pergona?"

He said: "A curious man. People say he was a priest. He never talks of himself. He sees no one. He speaks to nobody. He doesn't drink, he doesn't smoke, and all his money he spends on books or candles. At night, how many nights, when I wake up I see a candle burning and him praying on his knees."

104

The man was relieved from his post, and after that I saw him often walking in the ranks with a heavy pack on his back, smaller than his comrades, trying to keep pace with them, paler than usual, sweat streaming down his face, his black eyes burning like coals. There was something exalted, something passionate in him.

AIT KHARKAIT
November 10th

We never stay long in one place. The relief of outposts occurs as often as possible and this constant change of scenery and environment suits the nomadic nature of the legionnaire.

And so we are again on the road bound for the Taghzirt group of posts, which overlook the two rivers of Drent and Derna.

Yesterday morning we left Kasbah Tadla, the music going before and accompanying us to the outskirts of the town. At noon we were already approaching the outpost of Taghzirt, at the foot of the rocky mountain and opposite the hill where we had camped before. There had been the base of our former operations. All the group of posts that I will have under my command were created only last spring by my unit. Now we are to be in charge of the same posts, which are the most ad-

105

vanced in this region, and which overlook the native villages that have come under our protection.

I remember when we arrived there in the spring. The natives left their fields, their gardens, their villages, their kasbahs; some of them even burned their houses. But it took only a few months for these people to acquire confidence in us and to become friendly. They have begun anew their interrupted labors, and we have advanced to them enough wheat to sow the ground. What a joy now to see all the gardens carefully tended, as though they were children of a tender age! The fields were freshly plowed before being sown, and now one already sees the velvet of the green, which in the future will mean the daily bread of these Berbers.

One of my officers, riding beside me, said, "And just think, the Romans two thousand years ago passed along here. How old everything is and yet how young! . . . How everything renews itself! Yes, life is an eternal transformation. . . ."

The outpost is very large. It is divided into two parts. The larger part is inhabited by Arabs with their families. In order to protect this rich plain, upon which thousands of cattle are grazing, each one of the dozen tribes to whom it belongs send men, who with our men, protect this property from the mountain brigands. We help to arm these men, to equip them, and even to train them.

These natives who now protect the plains were formerly pillagers themselves and only a few years ago it was unsafe to travel in this country—not only for the white man, but for the natives. Everything lay in waste. There was general poverty, and no one dared to live in the open. One could not leave cattle in the fields during the night. The population was scattered here and there, living huddled in small fortified villages.

December 2nd

The annex to my post, where the native guard live with their families, is very picturesque. The women are dressed in varicolored garments and the men in blue burnouses which they put over white burnouses. The blue burnous is a sign that the man belongs to the regular guard. Mounted on their horses, which have long manes and long tails, with their multicolored and high saddles, with steel stirrups, engraved and encrusted with silver or with white metal, they are very vivid.

Communication with the rest of the posts in the group is by telephone in the daytime. But when the telephone is cut or is out of order we communicate by heliograph in Morse code in the daytime, and at night we signal with lanterns. The African air being very clear, signals can be seen many miles away.

Two rivers, very rapid and full, originating in the high mountains, flow on either side of the post. On the banks oleander is growing and the waters are full of fish. Here and there a luxurious palm tree reaches toward the sky.

January 5, 1924

In military life more than elsewhere everybody must take his chance. It does no good to remain in the rear. It does not pay to be more careful than is needful. No one can escape his destiny.

I have just lost an adjutant in my company. It is a great pity. Somebody had to get the bullet he received, and perhaps it was his day. Poor Duval! He was very gay and bright, rather small and delicate looking, and yet a strong, sturdy soldier, who, in spite of two wounds and being gassed in the Great War, was one of the best noncommissioned officers of the battalion. The men liked him. They gladly went with him wherever he led, and never was there trouble in his section.

His outpost was the only one not to be relieved with the others. I disliked to leave him there be-

102

cause it was his right to be relieved, but I had definite orders to keep him in his post, as no soldiers were available to replace his men. I had a premonition that something was going to happen to him. My intuition did not fail.

Last night—a clear night with a full moon, almost as bright as day—a legionnaire sentry was standing on a bastion overlooking the country. One has to be careful standing there in the middle of the night. It is at that time the nocturnal prowlers descend from the mountains to rove around, to try to get something—a sheep that the natives have forgotten to put inside the walls of their village, a horse that has escaped, or a mule. Often they come and lie quietly in the vicinity of the post, hoping to get something at daybreak if not during the night. A sentry becomes sleepy after an hour of watching. Then the brigand who is spying on him swings a rope; and there have been occasions when men were pulled from the bastion with their guns, sometimes killed, sometimes not, but always robbed of everything they had.

In order to find out whether a sentry is asleep, the natives throw stones against the bastion. Sometimes even though the sentry is not asleep, if he bends his head or sticks it out, immediately a rope swings and he is liable to receive it around his neck.

109

Of course we were aware of the tricks of the brigands, and in giving instructions to the sentries, we always warned them not to pay any attention to stones that might be thrown, and never to lean out of the tower.

But sometimes curiosity is stronger than orders, and this night the sentry, who perhaps had heard a noise in the barbed-wire fence around the post, inopportunely leaned out and was pulled down by invisible hands. He had only time to cry out. A sentry on another bastion sounded the alarm. Duval, who commanded the outpost, came out of his lodging and jumped on the bastion from which the man had disappeared, with a few men following him. He also leaned out to see what had become of the man. He received a bullet in his head. All covered with blood he was taken to his lodging and a man trained in first aid dressed his wound. He died the next morning.

Life is cruel, very often, and we have to have strength in order not to cry out against the injustice that falls upon us sometimes. But there must be a supreme and immanent justice which our limited intelligence cannot perceive or reach. I believe in a law of Supreme Equilibrium, which reconciles all things. In the sphere of individual affairs, God has nothing to do. He sees only the great systems which he has tuned with His sublime harmony. There are human beings who feel the current of the Great Life. They are happy and calm. There are others who revolt against what is implacable. They perish. There are also in this Great Life human beings who see beyond what it is permitted most of us to see. There are others who with their genius and activity try to hinder the order of the Great Life. They disappear.

In great love there is suffering and in every joy there is sadness. In friendship there is forgetfulness and a very great happiness always brings unhappiness. After fat years there are lean years. Only the one who acquires an understanding of the Harmony of the Cosmic Life attains calm and happiness.

January 20th

Yesterday one legionnaire was killed and another wounded, and their arms and two mules taken away while they were going to the river for water. Both were stabbed with daggers. By the time the post was aroused the brigands had disappeared into the mountains.

There was no priest in the vicinity to perform the last rites, and, therefore, one had to assume the obligation of sending these men to their eternal rest

111

as best one could. All the men of the outpost lined up around the graves where their comrades were to be buried. Then words of farewell were pronounced by the commanding officer.

X

A SON OF KINGS

AIT KHARKAIT
February 10, 1924

TO-DAY I received a telephone call from the Chief-of-Staff of Tadla asking me whether I thought the convoy of foodstuffs and munitions could start from Tadla to my post and whether the trails to the advance posts in the mountains were good enough and safe enough for the convoy to travel over. I told him that it was possible for it to come.

We waited for the convoy all day, and only with the approach of evening did the outlook in the tower signal that there was movement on the road below. The day was gray and heavy. Clouds were gathering all over the sky. I feared that the night would be bad, and was also apprehensive for the following day. The convoy came nearer and nearer, but already it was beginning to get dark. I put groups of men on the outlook, and sent a small detachment to meet them and help them safely to the place.

When they arrived there were more than three hundred mules, packed with all kinds of foodstuffs and with cases of munitions. The muleteers were tall Senegalese, tired and almost exhausted. These tall and dark soldiers of Senegal do not have the same endurance as Europeans, not even half the endurance of the Moroccans or the Algerians, who always find energy to pull themselves together and to meet circumstances in a more manly way.

This convoy was in charge of a Senegalese officer, a descendant of kings, the great-grandson of King Samory. He, speaking their language and knowing them thoroughly, had their confidence; and they, accepting him and knowing him as one of their own, obeyed him. Everything went smoothly.

The sergeant and corporals of these muleteers were also Senegalese, of a caste higher than the ordinary muleteer. They also knew how to deal with the men. They did not shout and yell at them. They did not order them here and there. They spoke to them quietly. After taking my instructions as to the locations and as to the way in which I thought it would be best to place both the men and the animals, the officer in command gave orders to unpack the mules.

Just as I feared, raindrops began to fall. While the unpacking proceeded, I went with the Senegalese lieutenant to show him the huts where his men were to be placed for the night. They were in the annex to our post, where the native guards lived with their

114

families. The lieutenant entered each hut. With his flashlight he would light it up, note its capacity, see in what condition it was, and then he would speak to a sergeant who accompanied him. When this was done, he detailed men to clean up the huts, and he asked me whether there was firewood to warm the night shelter of his men.

He was the first Senegalese lieutenant in command of a company made up of men of his own race that I had ever seen. And it was the first time I ever saw Senegalese soldiers do things quickly and without confusion.

While some of them attended to the mules, giving them food and putting straw before them, others started fires and began to cook their rice. The Senegalese have special food. They do not draw the regular rations of the army. Their rations consist chiefly of rice, but, of course, they have their ration of bread, coffee, sugar, lard, salt and meat.

Darkness had already fallen on the post, and in the large courtyard one saw these tall, black men, wrapped in blankets, gathering around the fires, and the light reflected strangely on their faces. They were quiet. I never heard them sing. They listened always to some one in a group who talked rapidly, and the language resembled the chirping or twittering of birds.

115

I invited Lieutenant Samory to be my guest. A room next to mine was given to him, and I told my Russian orderly to place himself at the disposal of the lieutenant and to make him comfortable. I saw a look of hesitation in the gray eyes of my orderly.

"What is the matter?" I asked.

"Nothing, nothing," he replied.

Then a long pause. "How black the lieutenant looks," he remarked.

"He doesn't *look* black. He *is* black. What next? What are you thinking? That you cannot help a black officer?"

He said nothing. He turned and went on with his work. After the lieutenant left the next morning my orderly while helping in the room said:

"But they are not savages. He is more of a gentleman than many. I have helped so many of those who come in charge of convoys. In the morning when they go sometimes they do not even look at you. But he thanked me. He went into the kitchen and he thanked the cook that cooked our dinner yesterday and he offered gifts to every one. We refused, of course. But think of a black man proposing gifts to us!"

February 12th

A convoy stopping at the outpost is a great resource for the Legion. While the legionnaire does not usually steal for himself, and never steals from his officers, he will take pride in stealing something which is of use to his unit.

In the morning when the Senegalese were about to leave the post they were astonished to see that the harness and the pack saddles did not fit their animals. Not only that, but most of the harness and the saddles were old. When they arrived yesterday they were all brand-new. The mules were the same in number, but some of them had become smaller and weaker during the night. They did not look the same as before. A complete transformation had taken place. I do not know whether the Senegalese lieutenant noticed these changes or not. I myself would not have known what had happened if the sergeant in charge of our mules, while making his daily report, had not told me.

"I reported to you a few weeks ago," he said, "about the bad condition of our pack equipment. Now I can report to you that nothing is missing and everything is new."

"What do you mean?" I asked. "We have not received any."

"No, we have not received any, but we have gotten it. We had to get it. We asked the commissariat several times to replace our equipment. There was

117

never any answer. We had to change it. What better opportunity could we have waited for? We have replaced everything. The Senegalese have the old. We have the new."

I reprimanded him, but he said:

"I did not order it done. The men did it themselves—the legionnaires—each one for his mule. They have been waiting for this chance for a long time. And, after all, it is not for ourselves, it is for the good of the service."

Stealing a mule from another unit is a complicated affair. All the mules are branded with a number on the hoof: so the number has to be changed. The mules are of different colors: they have to be painted! Nothing stops the legionnaire!

The legionnaire never lacks for material or for food. When he goes to the commissariat to get a supply of oats he always takes additional sacks and the mules of the Legion are well fed. When he goes for sugar or coffee he always tries to embroil the clerk in charge in an argument in order to get more than he should receive. When he is to get fifteen head of livestock for butchering, he always tries to take two or three heads more. All this, he claims, is for the good of the unit. Punishments are inflicted now and again on the legionnaires. They take the punishment, but that never stops them.

118

Passing a flock of sheep, they always try to slip two or three lambs under their clothes or into the pack on their mules. Amid the silence of the road I would hear sometimes the baa-a-a, baa-a-a of sheep and I would go to see where it came from. Discovering the little lambs I would start to question the men. Nobody ever knew where they came from. Nobody brought them. Nobody had seen them come.

March 10th

After a few days of rain, the sun has once more reappeared. All the fields and the valleys, as if awakening from sleep, have come to life. Some of the hills are shining with the golden yellow flowers that cover them. Such a wonderful, fantastic, velvet carpet! No man's hand and no human imagination could have created such a complexity of form and variety of color. The mountains which drop abruptly into the valley are covered with a blue veil and after midday the rays of the sun envelop with a shining web the ravines between the mountains. Below the height on which the white fortress is standing two rivers join and flow rapidly to the west, watering the rich and fertile plain of Tadla. All that plain now is plowed. The fields are beginning to be covered with green and are becoming more beautiful with each passing day. A few days

119

ago the peasants, clad in long white shirts, began to rake over the 'unplowed earth, and in a few days it will be fecund with the seeds of corn.

I come every day to the edge of the hill to breathe the fresh morning air. I turn my face toward the wind, and breathe deeply. This air which is so strong and full of life!

On the other side of the river there are terraces of gardens, wonderfully arranged, climbing to the mountains. The fruit trees that were abandoned last year when the inhabitants, fearing our arrival, left the place and went into the mountains, are now trimmed and pruned and banded. All the ground between the trees has been cleaned up and fences of gray, thorny shrubs are guarding the entrance to these heavenly groves. Oranges, lemons, the sweetest perfumed tangerines, almonds, peaches, apricots, pomegranates, figs, are growing here, and between the trees vines are climbing, clinging to their trunks. There are not many palm trees here. One date palm, with its straight, slender trunk, grows high into air and makes still more rich this picturesque amphitheater, which comes close to the mountain slopes full of dark openings and grottoes of most peculiar form. In these grottoes, resting from the burning sun, are flocks of sheep tended by young shepherd boys in white burnouses.

120

XI

THE CAID GIVES A FEAST

AÏT KHARKAIT

March 15, 1924

I WAS invited to-day to a feast given by the Caid of the region. In an orange grove on a cleared place on the grass, carpets were spread. There were two big carpets where fifty men could sit easily. On these carpets cushions of the most striking colors were thrown. Then further on there were grass mats laid on the ground. We arrived rather early. In the village we were met by the elder men of the tribe in snow-white attire and with snow-white turbans. We left our horses and escort in the village. We laid aside our arms, and accompanied by these older men and by other guests we went into the grove. The Caid himself met us, but he did not follow, because he had to supervise the roasting of the mutton, of the chickens, of the wild game, and look after the sweets that were being prepared for his guests.

Slowly the guests assemble. Here I see coming a tall old man, the beautiful Maho-Roha, on his head a white turban, and a striking blue caftan is seen under his thin white burnous. He walks with a decided step, and his strong, muscular feet are dressed in embroidered leather slippers. He is swinging his arms and throwing out his chest and stomach, because a large stomach is a sign of prosperity. When a man has a large stomach it means that heaven has smiled upon him—he is very rich, that he eats well and that he is not obliged to work, having many servants to work for him.

Just behind him comes another man, very small, tripping along with tiny steps, clad in a gray burnous and wearing spectacles. He is thin and has a pale face surrounded by a fringe of brown beard. While tripping along he constantly arranges his spectacles. This is the *fki* or learned man, the scribe of the Caid. He is the trustee of all the secrets of the house. He writes most elaborate and verbose letters. Also he prepares the tea for the guests the Caid receives, because preparing tea is one of the most honorable positions in the house. And especially is he in the house of the Caid to lead the conversation. In order to show others that he is the advisor of the Caid, now and then he will whisper something in the ear of his patron. He does not say a word even—he only wants us to believe that he is telling secrets to his master—to show that he is

122

in his confidence. Everybody, of course, under-stands the trick and yet after the whispering we all look at him approvingly, nodding our heads as if to say, "Oh, yes, we understand how confidential you are with the Caid."

Here is another Caid, Bou Adi, alighting from his horse. He is a man middle-aged, with a short neck and an absolutely round head, all shaved. He is dark. He has a big mouth with thick lips and a flat nose. A black beard surrounds his face as with a ring. He has big, thick brows and dark, intelli-gent eyes which are shining with a strange light.

He is followed by his brother, a thoughtful man, who when walking is always turning his head as if looking for some one.

And then there comes Caid Ben Nasser. He came from the mountains not long ago, and after that the whole region surrendered itself to the Central Government of Morocco. He came with more than one hundred tents, women and children, herds of sheep, cows and oxen. His father, one of the fiercest of brigands, died not long ago, and now his son is the most influential man in the mountains. His coming into our lines is a great tribute to our policy of peaceful penetration into the mountainous Berber country. It also means security for the tribes living

123

on the plains. From now on they will not fear the brigands.

Ben Nasser walks easily, lightly. One feels his great strength. Everything about him is powerful; force breathes from him. One feels that no matter what this man had to do it would be easy for him. He is not richly clad. His gray caftan is homespun of thick wool. His burnous is also of thick gray wool and instead of a turban he wears a twisted red band around his head, knotted at the back.

Now Ali El Luli arrives—small, fat, with a broad smile on his face. He is the chief of a rich tribe. He is clever, tricky. He is keen to dominate everybody and everything. He has taken under his protection all the villages and dwellings of the peasants. He is buying up all their crops. He has made a wide road to his kasbah, where all the grain is being stored, and he is doing a great trade with the near by towns.

Others, many of them, arrive, dismounting from their horses, which are taken away by their servants. The young men of the village are coming and the children also come to the grove where the feast is being held.

On one side of the big carpet, where many cushions are thrown one upon another, the most honored guests are sitting. They are not speaking loudly.

124

They do not talk much. Those who sit on the carpets look from one to another. Now and then, very quietly, they say a word. And the answers are not hasty. One thinks before one speaks. There is slow, deliberate conversation. They make no gestures, and their faces are impassive. They are speaking about the sowing, discussing the number of cattle that they possess, what is being done in the mountains, what they are intending to do next spring, talking about the chiefs of tribes in the mountains who intend to come and live peacefully under the Sultan.

On the straw mats around our carpet men of less importance are sitting. And finally the different foods arrive. One after another tall, thin negroes appear, slaves for generations to the big Caids, their ancestors having been brought here from the Soudan by the Sultan Mula Y Ishmail in the seventh century. These negroes carry on outstretched hands enormous round bowls filled with food. Others are bringing low, round tables on which are placed whole sheep on spits. Still others are bringing plates of fruit and sweets. And then other servants come with braziers filled with live coals to keep the food hot.

Finally the host himself appears, wearing a rose caftan, over which is a white burnous of silk muslin.

He steps on the carpet, and advancing to each of the important guests, bows to him and begs to apologize that the food perhaps may not be to his taste. Then clapping his hands he makes a sign for the slaves to come forward. He himself does not sit among the honored guests, but goes to the farthest end of the carpet, from which the food is being brought. He directs the succession of the different plates to be put before his guests.

He himself appears to be the most humble person in the whole assembly. Now and again, when something is being served, he comes forward with reverent bows and pulls out with his finger the best piece of mutton or chicken or whatever it may be and he gives it now to one important guest, now to another. Sometimes he himself tastes a piece of chicken or mutton, and then goes again to his corner and directs the serving.

When the low, round tables are brought six or seven men draw up their cushions and seat themselves around each table, forming most picturesque groups. No knives or forks are used, and one uses only the fingers of the right hand. The left hand is never used.

First the roast mutton is served, then the chicken. We begin the chicken courses with roast chicken with sweet potatoes. Then comes chicken

126

in a highly spiced sauce with sweet peppers. After that chicken in a rather gray sauce with raisins in it. Then come different kinds of lamb stew with all sorts of vegetables. After that comes the *kouskous* (a pudding which may be one of two kinds: one is sweet with raisins and the other made of corn and meat and is boiled in the juice of meats). Afterwards come the sweets. There are cakes made in thin layers, with cinnamon and sugar sprinkled on top, and many cakes of different kinds made of almond flour.

Of all the food that is served only the best parts of the sheep or the chicken are consumed by the honored guests. Then the same plate goes to a guest of less importance. The guest of less importance eats only a certain part of what remains and then it goes to the dependents of the invited guests. From the dependents it goes to the men in service of the different guests—their military escort, their armed men—and after they have eaten it goes to the women in the village, and finally the bones are thrown to the dogs.

When the food has been taken away the servants come with brass and copper trays on which are pitchers and bowls, with towels and soap, for washing the hands. While washing his hands every guest tries to show contentment and pleasure in the food by hiccoughs, the louder the better. It is to show the host that the meal is excellent, that everybody is greatly satisfied.

Then tea is served. Here comes an old, old man with white hair and a long white beard. He is clad in a green caftan with a white burnous over it. He sits down in the middle of the big carpet, and several shining copper trays with teapots and glassware are put before him. Then, in a white napkin, which is tied in a bundle, tea is brought to him. Sugar in the form of a cone is also brought. He unties the tea, smells it, takes handfuls of it out of the bundle, smells it again. There are several pots, as there are many people. In each pot he puts a handful of tea. Then with a hammer he knocks off, from the big cone of sugar, a few pieces, and puts them into the pots. There is still another white bundle that has been put before him, containing mint. This he unties also, and takes out the mint leaves, which he rubs together between his hands, smells them, and puts a small quantity into each pot.

Near by is a servant beside a brazier fanning the coals on which a teakettle is standing. The old man makes a sign to the servant, who pours water into the different teapots where the mixtures have been put. After the teapots have been filled with water, the old man fills three or four glasses from each pot. He tries them, then puts them again into the same pot, tries again, and finally when he thinks it to be to the taste of the honorable guests, he fills up all the glasses. Servants come, take up the trays on which the glasses are set, and offer the tea to the guests.

By this time, on account of the heat and the amount of food that everybody has eaten, not much conversation is being carried on. Everybody is rather sleepy. Some of the old men are fast asleep and snoring, and are being kicked about by their neighbors in order to waken them.

The tea is drunk in a very loud manner. While taking the tea from the glasses men inhale it with a very obvious sound, with much smacking of the lips. The host watches everybody. He is contented when he sees that the guests are hiccoughing and smacking their lips.

Compliments are made always to the one who makes the tea. They say the tea has a very good aroma. "Tea without the aroma of mint is like a Caid without servants." To which others reply, "A courageous Caid goes alone to battle and needs no bodyguard, and good tea needs no mint for its aroma."

After the tea, one guest after another begins to

129

leave, saying good-by to the host and telling him how rich his feast was, and that there was an abundance of everything.

March 20th

When early in the morning my orderly knocks at the door to tell me that my horse is ready and waiting, he comes in with a bouquet of flowers that he has picked on the road. Every time he goes to water the horse he gathers flowers for me, and sometimes he changes them twice a day. He is a Cossack from the steppes of the Don River, and he tells me that they have the same flowers there. He knocks on my door, opens it, takes off his kepi, and stands at attention, his bouquet in his hand. Then he coughs shyly and says:

"I have the honor to declare to you that the weather is very good."

I tell him that I am happy that the weather is very good, and then he comes into the room and takes away the old flowers, puts water in the vase, and arranges the fresh flowers in it. He never fails to say how beautiful the flowers are here. "But," he interpolates, "we have the same in my country," and then his eyes always become wet. He blushes, and is silent. I understand him well, this poor Cossack in Africa, so far away from home.

130

March 22nd

We have many children here of the natives who live in the annex to the post. I watch them often.

Children are everywhere the same. I have always observed that until a certain age of human beings, no matter of what race or color they may be, their interests, their games, their joys and sorrows are always the same. They have the same amusements as the children of Europe or America. With the same intonations they express their sorrow and happiness, their surprise and doubt. Just like other children they are very curious and scoffing. They are without pity for the older people, and like other children, their happiness or sorrow passes by quickly. Just as no one teaches little dogs and calves to jump, or to be surprised by their own feats, or by their growing strength, or by anything that surrounds them, no one teaches these children.

They grow, and according to the measure of their growth they adapt themselves to the life that is shaped around them by the adult children who are their parents, for the natives in this solitary settlement in the mountains live as unconsciously as children to the end of their days.

I often stop to watch these dark children in dirty, gray woolen burnouses. They build little carriages, making wheels out of the cactus that grows there. They make tops which they spin. They play hopscotch. They build fortresses on the ground. They make fires. They play hide-and-seek. Or holding hands they march around in a circle singing. They make dolls out of rags—they paint their eyes and ears, they tattoo their faces, and put a cloth around them—and the little girls mother them as if they were children.

I often see the boys and girls drawing, in a toy cart made of pieces of tin, the four-year-old grandson of the shaush, or chief, of the native troops in the fortress. This youngster gives orders to the human horses, imitating in tone the commands that are given by his grandfather, who is beaming with pleasure at the sight of his grandchild so entertained by his playmates. At sunset, before the gates of the post are closed, one sees this old man, who generally looks so fierce and savage, walking about and playing with the child in his arms, filled with tenderness and good nature.

Boys at the age of five or six already attend to the horses of their fathers. They jump on their backs and ride down to the river to water. The children's heads are shaved with the exception of a short lock of hair. They believe that by this lock the child will be pulled into heaven.

132

The children make turbans of wild flowers and wonderful crowns of red poppies, which are extremely large here. It is wonderful to see these dark children on a carpet of flowers, under the bright sun, with their red crowns on their heads.

April 12th

I notice with myself and with others, also, that we are all more peaceful, more quiescent, when the sun retires on the other side of the horizon. A certain relaxation overtakes one's soul. People, like objects, change at the end of the day. The objects that we call dead, the matter that appears to our limited vision to be without soul, how intensively it now seems to live!

Here the old kasbah stands, with its walls high and severe. At this moment the Arabs in white burnounses are coming from the fields. The shepherds are bringing in their flocks. All of them will return tired and weary from their long day in the sun. They come with heads down and pass by the walls of the kasbah.

Look at this tower, high and square and strong. How red it is, almost of ocher and gold! It emanates a breath of life. One would say that the walls do not reflect the light of the setting sun—that they do not receive the light, but, on the contrary, they give

133

out light, they are illuminated from within with a light fantastic and mysterious.

All things speak, all things are unfolding and then closing, living their own life in these wonderful hours of the evening. Centuries are passing, civilizations are being effaced. In relation to Eternal Things what is our short life, so full of pride and conceit—so small, so insignificant beside the ages that have passed away into human forgetfulness? What do we understand of all the mysteries that surround us?

BOOK II

MOROCCO

SPAIN
GIBRALTAR
Straits of Gibraltar
TANGIER
CEUTA
INTERNATIONAL ZONE
TETUA
SPANISH

ATLANTIC OCEAN

Oued

MEHDIA
RABAT
FEZ
MEKNÈS
CASABLANCA
MAZAGAN

Oued Oum Rbia

Boujad

SAFI

K^{ba} TADLA
Ksiba (Kseibat)
Rhorm el Alem
Alemsid
Timoulilt
Tri Pnin
K^{ba} Mellal
Oued el Abid
Azilal

MOGADOR
MARRAKECH

ATLAS MO

AGADIR

FRENCH PROTECTORATE

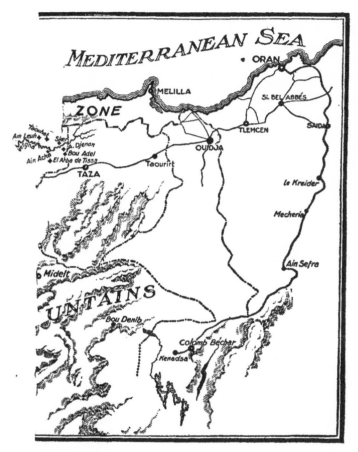

MEDITERRANEAN SEA

ORAN

MELILLA

ZONE

Si. BEL ABBÉS

Taouna
Ain Leuh
Sejer
Sidi
A. Djenan
Bou Adel
Ain Acha
El Aba de Tissa
TAZA

Taourirt

OUDJA

TLEMCEN

SAIDA

le Kreider

Mecheria

Ain Sefra

Midelt

UNTAINS

Bou Denib

Colomb Béchar

Kenadsa

OF MOROCCO

I

WE PREPARE FOR THE RIFF

ALGIERS. LE KREIDER
November 10, 1924

AFTER two years of campaigning in Morocco the legionnaires come to Algeria for a period of rest.

The Legion being essentially a fighting unit, the time spent in Algeria is employed chiefly in training the men for future campaigns and in instructing new recruits. Long marches are made both by night and by day. Camps are built in order to train the men to pitch their tents in the shortest possible time. All are instructed in the use of the different armaments that are needed in a campaign. Specialists are trained in every company—grenade-throwers, machine gunners, liaison men who learn how to communicate in the Morse code and how to employ the different signals used by the army. Telephone and telegraph operators are also trained.

But the legionnaire prefers to stay here as short a time as possible. He thinks this quiet existence as not in keeping with the spirit of a legionnaire, and

regards these months in Algeria as a sort of exile—
the dullest period of his life in the Legion.

I feel the charm of life here in the desert. Many
times I am sad because I have the feeling that I am
of no use in the world. The days go by and I have
done nothing, yet there is much to do, even here.

I try to perform my duty, and I expend my forces
in taking care of my men and in trying to be of use
to them. Everybody in this world needs sympathy.

December 5th

What solitude! What silence envelops me when
I ride out from the little town near which the battalion is located. I am in the middle of a desert of
sand. The changing dunes are buffeted by strong,
whirling winds which are ever moving them here and
there. They are never the same. From afar these
little hills resemble the waves of a sea whose motion
has been suspended by a magic spell.

When you stop your horse in the middle of this
ocean of sand, covered by the magnificent blue of the
sky, when all around there is nothing to break the
silence and peace, when the circle of the horizon seems
to touch the Infinite, you are overcome by a feeling of
admiration, of surprise and wonder before the great-
ness, the magnitude of nature . . . of life . . . of
existence.

140

It is very cold this evening. The night is clear. The moon is high overhead. The air is ringing and pure.

After the bugler sounds taps no noise comes to trouble the solemnity of the night.

January 11, 1925

For the last two days we have been in the turmoil of a sand storm which enveloped the men and animals and penetrated to every part of the houses. Even our mouths were filled with sand. Everything around is yellow and gray. For a few days before the storm we all felt inert, weak and nervous. We knew a storm was about to break.

My orderly came before dawn to open the shutters of the windows. As soon as they were thrown open I saw the red light of the newborn day. I stood there facing the east, full of emotion at the sight of this wonderful spectacle. The sun was rising and bringing with it the expected storm in a red veil of sand.

It was yet far away, but the silence of the air was shattered from time to time by wild bursts of wind that made everything tremble in its path. Not only the horizon in the east was aflame, but now the cupola of the heavens seemed alive in this fire kindled by a mysterious and unknown force.

141

Always before such a storm there is perfect still-
ness and calm at sunrise, but the unusual redness of
the dawn indicates the storm's approach. Nevertheless, we had to go out for a march.

We had been marching about two hours when
the wind began to blow harder and harder. Already
the men were advancing with great difficulty. My
horse, restless and blinded by the sand, became almost unmanageable. It began to whirl around and
envelop us, like a mist, and we could not see the
sky nor where we were going. We no longer walked
on firm ground, but on moving sand.

When we could not advance farther, we gathered
together in a circle and waited. As soon as it was
possible to move we went back to the fortification.
The return journey was very painful. We marched
as close together as possible, and the men in the rear
kept watch to see that no one was left behind. An
additional glass of wine compensated the men for
their efforts during the day.

The terrible sirocco had not stopped whistling,
and continued to throw itself against the fortification
with all its weight. It battered the walls and windows with terrific force, throwing wave after wave of
sand against them. We were like people besieged in
a fortress. The enemy was bombarding us—only in

142

this Algerian desert the enemy was the sand storm and the wild hurricane.

For two days the wind blew, bringing with it the sand from the desert, and life became almost unbearable. No one dared to go out. Not until the third day was everything calm again. Then the country seemed even more beautiful than before. Not a breath of air was stirring and every one was happy to be alive. Every man in the barracks was singing.

April 5th

It has been a long winter here in the desert. The men are tired of the quiet life, of being shut off from the rest of the world by the sea of sand, and seeing no one except their own units. Drill in the morning, drill in the afternon, then long marches for weeks—all that has become monotonous. But a few weeks ago everybody was stirred up because orders were issued to prepare the battalion for a campaign in Morocco. We are to be sent, together with other units, as reënforcements to relieve the outposts in northern Morocco which are surrounded by the Riffians.

Preparations were carried on most actively. All armaments were inspected and completed. A full examination of the clothing of the men was made, and by small groups, day after day, the men went to the

143

stores of the unit to receive a new outfit. Special attention was given to the shoes, because it is a most important thing that the shoes of the legionnaire, who has to march a great deal, shall fit exactly. Every commander of a unit places special stress upon this question, and all officers of the Legion know the feet of their men as well as they know their faces.

Just as soon as word was received that we were to go to Morocco every man had to pass a medical examination. Because of the hardships they would have to undergo, and because of the severe climate every legionnaire was tested as to his physical endurance and strength. Every illness that he had had or was now having was taken into account, and from the day of the examination the men in the units were divided as "fit" and "unfit" for the campaign.

There were a few cases where men of weak morale or weak physique would declare themselves to be even worse than they really were, claiming all kinds of illness. Their commander, knowing the hardships his unit would have to endure in the campaign, wanted to have around him not a quantity of men, but men of quality. And, therefore, anyone who perhaps was not very sick, but who maintained that he was sick, thereby showing his weak morale, was generally exempted from going into battle.

II

BABIN, THE OLD BUGLER

April 5, 1925

B ABIN, the old bugler, was declared unfit for the campaign. He would not believe it.

"But, *Monsieur le Major*, you honestly don't mean it. You are joking. What do you mean, I unfit? Am I old? Is that why? Or because I was wounded three times? Or because I had diarrhea for the last two weeks? No, really why? Your pardon, *Monsieur le Major*, but what is the matter with me? I can't remain here when everybody goes. Why, I am the old of the old, the oldest in the whole Legion . . . bugler to the most famous officers in the Legion, in the best companies of the Legion, every day for the last seventeen years. Will I have to remain here in the barracks? Here in the desert with a lot of weaklings who should be ashamed to call themselves legionnaires? Oh, no, *Monsieur le Major*, you can't put this over me . . . over the old Babin."

The doctor was tired and irritated, and the young Austrian legionnaire who acted as his aid had no use for Babin. And possibly he could not under-

145

stand, being softened by his easy job, why this old man insisted in wanting to be put on the fit list for the campaign in Morocco. He made a sign to Babin to leave, and called the next one. The old bugler remained awhile, saw that nobody paid any attention to him, standing there tottering, and:

"God! My God!" he said. "My God! Is this the Legion? Fit! Unfit! The sacred name of God! I am going to complain!"

He put on his kepi, pulled himself together, saluted, and turning on his heels in the regulation manner, made his way to the door. The young legionnaires jeered at him. He stopped and looked at them, his face working with rage.

"A lot of greenhorns and youngsters," he said, "a lot of fatimas, old women! And you call yourselves legionnaires!"

He rushed to the bureau, presented himself to the sergeant major and asked to see me. Sitting in an adjoining room, I overheard, and told him to come in. Babin entered, his chest forward. He was short, broad-shouldered, his face burned with the sun, with many wrinkles scratched on it, and cuts running long and wide. What a human map, what a history is written on that face! What history and adventure! Bringing his heels together, he saluted and stood at attention.

146

"*Repos,*" I said. "What is the matter?"

"Oh," he exclaimed, "something is wrong, sir. They declare I am unfit, I can't go with you. I, the bugler." On a three-colored, twisted cord hooked to his belt there was his bugle hanging. "I, the bugler," he went on, "to remain with this lot of youngsters, with this lot of weaklings! There is something wrong with the Legion! Why, before, before, the legionnaire was never asked whether he was too sick to march or not. Then he marched or he died. He was wounded . . . yes. He became sick while on a campaign, so sick as even to lose the light of day in his eyes . . . yes. Dropped dead with fatigue . . . yes. But only when he was dead was he released from service. And he always could make his death worth while, the old legionnaire! But now—oh, no, I simply can't bear it. There are fits and unfits for a campaign—they are too weak, too ill, the darlings. I would rather die than to live to see such a shameful thing!"

The old man trembled, his body was shaking, he ground his teeth and moaned. I stood up from my bench.

"Come here, old man, nearer to me. Come here. You know me, do you not? I tell you, you will go with me."

From that time on Babin was seen frequently

at the telephone station. He wanted to be the first to learn that the orders had come. He wanted to be first to sound the alarm, the *Rassemblement Générale*, the great call to start off for the unknown.[1]

April 8th

All the "unfit" were put in a special barrack under corporals also unfit to go to Morocco. Sergeants and officers were also tested. And these "unfit," both officers and men, were to remain in the fortress and take charge of it during the time that the unit would be away.

There was a certain contempt on the part of the "fit" toward the "unfit," although many of the men were really physically unfit and did not deserve this contempt. On the other hand, there was among the "unfit" a certain irony toward the outgoing men. The older ones who had endured many battles and were too weak and ill to go on another campaign assumed a rather superior air toward the young legionnaires, who were so zealous to leave the place and go to Morocco. They would say:

"Well, you will see. You will tell us afterwards how you have enjoyed it. We have done our share and we are glad to stay here. We shall be quiet.

---

[1] Babin did go with his company. And he fell, riddled with bullets, while sounding the Charge.

We shall have nothing to do. We shall have a wonderful time, while you will have all kinds of hardships there."

But when the day of the order to march came, when finally the war outfit and the war kits were completed, when those who were to go were all clad in new uniforms and assembled with their kits in the courtyard, then the "unfit," in their working suits, looked on with envy.

And many of them, many more than one could even expect, filed requests to go with their comrades. Men crowded into the offices of their commanders. With tears in their eyes they asked the sergeant major to present them to the captains. Even those who had claimed all kinds of sickness while not sick at all, or very slightly, would implore to be taken. And especially the old men, who were really unfit, those who had already endured great hardships, those who only last week had looked ironically at the younger men—they especially wanted to go. Many of them wept. They said:

"No, it's a shame, for me, an old legionnaire. Why, I am fit! I don't believe the doctor who examined me. He doesn't know me, because he did not take into account the spirit that will keep me going even if I am old and worn out."

Many of them were known personally to the commanding officers, and had fought in some of the engagements in Morocco. They would recall to their former chiefs these things:

"But haven't you seen me? Don't you know me—what I'm made of? Please, do let me go with you."

Nothing could be done. There are orders, there are rules, there is discipline in the Legion for every occasion. And it is because of this that a great unit composed of so many nationalities—all this assembly of young and old coming from the different parts of the earth—submit themselves to the rigid discipline of the Legion.

III

GOULET, THE "REAL GAUL"

April 12, 1925

GOULET was one of the oldest men in the company. In his military book where his *curriculum vitæ* was inscribed one could see that he had had a rather exciting career. Many times he was corporal, several times he was sergeant. Then again corporal, once more raised to sergeant, then reduced to a private. All these changes in his fortune were due to his weakness for drink. He would get drunk as often as he could afford it. Having seen more than ten years of service in the Legion, he was good at all kinds of professions and trades. When men were needed for one sort of work or another, Goulet always could be called upon. In building a post one day, when a mason fell ill, Goulet immediately was called to take his place. He made a good mason. When a muleteer was taken sick and someone was needed to replace him in the emergency, Goulet was there. When no bugler was available to go to an outpost, one thought of Goulet, and he became a bugler. When a telephone operator was needed temporarily, one sent for Goulet. He was experienced in all kinds of jobs, all sorts of work, in everything that a legionnaire could be called upon to do, and always he would prove himself capable and expert. Good-natured, good-humored, always friendly with everybody, quiet and placid when he was sober, he would become an absolute nuisance, a most disturbing element, when he had had a drink. And the reason? Afterwards when he was sober he would say to his commanding officer:

"Yes, I know. I know my weakness. I am paying for the sins of others, perhaps. My *maman* was a drunkard. My *papa* was a drunkard. How could you expect me to be otherwise than as I am?"

Such tenderness he put into these appellations, *papa* and *maman*. They were drunkards, but all the same they were his *papa* and *maman*.

One always could rely on Goulet if he gave his word. Never did he break it once it was pledged. One day he was very much excited. He had received news that a relative of his had died and left him an inheritance of 4,000 francs, a sum of money the value of which he could not even size up in wine and drinks. Four thousand francs! That meant, perhaps, one hundred years of a legionnaire's pay. It was overwhelming. It was almost too much for him. He began to borrow money, one franc, five francs, as much as he could. He went to the canteen, showed the letter advising him of his inheritance to the canteeneer, and got drinks on credit. But the money was slow in coming, and a week had passed since he received the astonishing letter. He wanted to continue to get credit, but everybody laughed at him and wondered to themselves how they could have believed that a man like Goulet ever could receive such a sum of money. Even he himself began to doubt whether it was not a joke on him, this great inheritance. But he thought that even if the inheritance did not come, already he had had a week of good times on the promise of it.

The money did arrive. And it arrived when the company was actively engaged in preparing itself to go to Morocco. He was called to the bureau of the company. He was asked to come to my office. Entering the room he saw on my desk a package of money. He turned pale. He almost trembled. He was asked to approach the table. I said:

"Here is your money, Goulet. I have the authority to give it to you now, or to withhold it and give it to you later in Morocco. And I did not even have to tell you the money was here. It is sent in care of me, but it is yours, and sooner or later you must receive it. You know that the company is being prepared to go to Morocco. Within

153

a few days we shall start off. We shall have to cross Algeria. We shall go through as legionnaires and show ourselves as we really are—quiet and disciplined. I know you and your weakness. If I give you this money you will want to spend it. You will spend it on the road. I know that you will share everything with your comrades, and finally everybody will be drunk. You must promise me that if I give you this money everything will be all right —that there will be no disturbance. Of course, I shall take measures to prevent it, but still I want you to share the responsibility for your unit."

Goulet went pale. His chin quivered. In a low voice he said:

"I give my word that you will have no trouble with me or my comrades on account of this money."

I handed it to him. He could not count it, his hands were trembling so. Again and again he tried, but he could not. I counted it for him and he went away with all the money in his hands, wondering what he should do with it.

The sergeant major, coming in the evening to my office, said:

"I have many papers for your signature to-day. There are about sixty permissions of leave until midnight to be signed."

As it was a weekday and no one was supposed to

leave the barracks, I asked, "Why, what is going on? Is there a traveling moving picture that the men want to see?"

He smiled ironically and said: "No, it is Monsieur Goulet who is giving a feast."

"Where?"

"At Madame Joannot's. You know——the widow who owns the little restaurant. He is giving a dinner there for sixty persons. He almost bought out the whole place——all that this poor woman had in her grocery even. She has started to collect dishes and utensils to set the table. There is excitement among all the canteen keepers who are struggling to see who will be in possession of Goulet's money twenty-four hours from now. I hope, sir, you will not sign these permissions."

"Where are they?"

The sergeant major presented a folder filled with small sheets of paper on which were written the names of the legionnaires who had asked for leave.

"I am going to sign," I told him. "Let them have their feast. I would rather they had it to-night than on the road."

The sergeant major stood up. "I beg your pardon, sir, I am an old legionnaire myself. You had better not sign them."

I looked at him. "I know what I am doing. Put

155

this order in your order book for to-night: 'Sixty legionnaires are permitted to go out of the camp and they must be back at five minutes to twelve. A special patrol composed of a sergeant, two corporals and twenty men will be assigned to duty from ten until twelve with instructions to have all the legionnaires back from the village at twelve o'clock sharp. At midnight not a sound is to be heard in the camp and not one light seen. The sergeant will be responsible for the execution of these orders.' "

Then Goulet was called again to the office and he was read the orders given for that night.

"You will have no trouble," he said. "Even if there were no patrol, Goulet himself would bring in any man who would be on the road."

Goulet kept his word. There was a great feast that night. Cases of champagne were opened. All the men had the time of their lives and at midnight everything was quiet in the barracks.

In the morning Goulet asked to see me. Handing me a thousand-franc bill, he said:

"Please, take it away from me. Here is an address. I ask that this sum be sent to the person whose name I have written on this paper."

"How much money do you have left, Goulet?" I asked.

156

"Three hundred francs."

We looked at one another understandingly. Goulet saluted and went out.

On the way to Morocco the freight car in which Goulet was traveling with his comrades was all decorated with branches of trees and in large letters written in chalk were these words: *"Voici le char des vrais legionnaires, des vrais Gaulois!"*

IV

ON THE WAY TO THE RIFF

April 13, 1925

THE order to march came suddenly—on a Sunday when everybody was quiet. The men were playing football and other games on the grounds around the barracks and the officers were in the mess or resting in their rooms.

The buglers, after sounding the *Rassemblement Générale* in the barracks, went out to the western gate of the fortification and sounded the alarm to the west, marched to the north and sounded it—to the east and to the south—in all directions, to all corners of the open space the bugle sounded. Everybody knew that it was the signal for departure, and according to the plans of mobilization, ten hours after the time the orders were received the unit was to march off.

And from the barracks, from the fields, from the grounds near by, from the desert for a mile around where there were groups of soldiers or isolated men, from the creek that was running not far from the fortifications where all the animals of the unit were,

158

from everywhere men ran to their respective places.

Immediately the men assembled in the barracks and the roll was called. Every corporal and sergeant has a book in which the names of all the men who are to march with him are inscribed, and also a record of the armament and outfit that has been assigned to each man to carry with him.

This was the end of a dreary and weary life in the barracks. Everybody was glad of the change, happy also to meet other men, other faces than those to which they were so accustomed. Glad to get away from the desert! They will meet other units. There will be marches in the mountains. They will see new countries, will have new environments. There is nothing the legionnaire loves more than changing his surroundings, marching, seeing new places. That is where he finds his wonderful morale. It is then that he can forget himself, his past life, his troubles, everything he wants to forget, and it is then he is inspired to adventure, which is the very essence of his nature. It is in action—in march or in battle—in struggling with nature and men that he is happiest.

In ten hours after the order came we were ready to go.

Everybody was in his place, and as instructions

159

had been given beforehand to every unit and to every section or group in a unit, we all knew exactly what to do.

Pay had to be given out to the men and officers; and then all accounts had to be closed; everything worked as regularly as a machine.

In the kitchens, hurriedly, the last meal to be eaten in the barracks was being prepared, and everything that the supply store or the magazine possessed was thrown into the kettle for the evening meal, that the men might have their pail full. Loaves of bread were distributed to last for the next day and a cold meal for the next morning.

Then all the kits, packed in their sacks, together with the rifles, were brought into the courtyard and every section and every unit arranged them in order in the place that had been assigned to it. Their supply of cartridges was distributed to the men.

Afterwards the sergeant quartermaster distributed reserve food. This food reserve consisted of two tins, one pound each, of corned beef and twelve biscuits, which were put in a tin box provided for the purpose. Salt and sugar and coffee were distributed, put in small sacks specially made for them, and then placed in the same box with the biscuits.

The complete outfit of the legionnaire was put in-

160

side a sack according to prescribed rules.[1] The
Legion sack has a wooden frame, and notwithstanding the variety of articles it contains, it is so tightly
packed that nothing can be displaced while the men
are marching, or even if the sack were to be thrown
onto the ground. Each article has its place and
always has to be put in the same place. Whenever
there is inspection of the contents of the sack, no
matter what time of day or night, no matter under
what circumstances, everything must be found in
its right place, and folded in the same way. Therefore, notwithstanding the small size of this walking
trunk and the quantity of different articles that it
contains, the legionnaire, because everything is in
order, can always find the thing he needs.

The additional pair of shoes is not placed inside
the sack, but with the slippers fastened to the outside, and over them is strapped the blanket wrapped
in that portion of the tent assigned to each man.
At the side of the sack were also strapped the tent
pegs and collapsible tent poles. Besides all this

[1] The sack contains a pair of new underdrawers, two new
shirts, one pair of socks, two handkerchiefs, two new neckties,
two new suits of clothes—one of cotton and one of wool khaki—
two towels, piece of soap, brush for the clothes, brush for the
shoes, brush for the rifles, spoon and fork, tin dish and tin cup,
a sewing kit, a new pair of shoes and a pair of slippers. Packages of surgical dressings are given out also, and they are put
into the coat pockets of the men.

161

every man had a portable tool to carry—an ax, a shovel, a pick, a saw. And then came the kitchen utensils. They also had to be carried by the men, and each was responsible for the utensil given to him. There were even coffee mills taken along. Each man had a blue or gray woolen sash, about four yards long, to wind around his body to protect him from the changes in temperature.

April 15th

A narrow-gauge railway ran within seven miles of the fortification, and railway carriages had been prepared to carry the men through Algeria to the Moroccan frontier. At five o'clock in the afternoon everything was ready, everything cleared up, and the legionnaires were finally assembled in the principal courtyard of the barracks. Before the command to march was given they were standing in groups, chatting. Only when, for the last time, the bugle sounded *Rassemblement*, did the men fall into ranks.

Finally the command came again: *"Garde à vous!"* and then, *"En avant, March!"* As soon as these words were shouted, the buglers, the fifers and the drummers assembled before the company at a distance of ten yards and started the pace with the "March of the Legion."

162

For many of the men it was the beginning of their last march.

In the morning early, immediately after sunrise, we entrained.

April 18th

During the two days that we have been traveling in Algeria we have gone through a magnificent country with forests and hills, its richly cultivated valleys where the green leaves of the vineyards are already in full display, where in these early days of spring all the fruit trees are in blossom. The white blossoms of the apple trees and the cherry trees look like brides, while the pink blossoms of the peach and apricot trees make one think of bridesmaids. In all the towns we passed through and in which we stopped the authorities and the population came to the stations to see us off. The legionnaires for a long time had not shown themselves in this part of the country.

In one of the principal cities where we had to stay six hours we were asked to parade. There is nothing that a legionnaire likes more than to parade, to be admired by the population, by the men and women—especially by the women and girls of the towns. It is one of the satisfactions, one of the innocent compensations, which the legionnaire has dur-

163

ing his hard and obscure life. It is the natural
appreciation and admiration of the civilian for the
legionnaire. With our own music we marched
through the town. The men were literally covered
with flowers thrown to them from balconies, and
when they were again in their carriages the population struggled to get into the station to bring
them all kinds of food and drink. During these two
days the acclamation of the inhabitants of Algeria
never ceased and all the legionnaires were in a most
gay and exultant mood.

April 20th

We are approaching Sidi-Bel-Abbes, which is the
mother town of the Legion. That is where all the
recruits for the Legion come. That is where they
abandon their civilian clothes for at least five years.
That is where they are first initiated into the spirit
of the Legion. That is where they start their first
maneuvers, their first hardships, their first contact
with the rules and regulations, with the customs and
habits of the Legion, with the old legionnaires, who
tell them about their former exploits.

At the station of this town the famous band of
the Foreign Legion, known all through Algeria,
was waiting for the train to arrive. This band
contains among its members men who have grad-

uated from the most famous conservatories of the world—men who have abandoned their profession for reasons unknown, and who are now simply soldiers in the rank and file like all the others.

It seems that the events through which they pass and the circumstances of their lives are particularly favorable to the development of their artistic faculties. Having no longer to concern themselves with the difficulties of making a living they can give themselves completely to their inner life. This life is enriched by all that passes before their eyes—the beauty of the landscape, the majesty of the desert, the heroism of the men—all mingled with their nostalgias and the memories of old sufferings.

An orchestra composed of musicians such as these is capable of evoking the deepest emotions; for they put into their music more dreams, more regrets, more yearning than are ordinarily to be found in the human heart.

When they play the "March of the Legion," so poignant and so martial, which expresses the rhythm of the march of the battalions, sometimes a great sadness comes over the legionnaire advancing along the dusty road . . . and a great pride as well. . . . They translate all the emotions of these men who have a past so rich and so tormented. The March is the soul of the Legion.

Marche de la Légion Étrangère
(March of the Foreign Legion)

April 22nd

The last big station before coming to the Moroccan frontier was at Tlemcen. Tlemcen has a garrison of Algerian sharpshooters, infantry and cavalry. At the station these Algerian troops were all lined up waiting for the coming train, very picturesque in their red and white burnouses and turbans. The native music of these troops saluted the Legion and the Legion replied by playing first the native regiment's tune and then that of the legionnaires.

Passing through Algeria, through this wonderfully peaceful country, it seemed strange to think that somewhere men had to fight again—that there could be trouble in this rich country where men had the opportunity to enjoy everything that life could give them. It was not until we reached Tlemcen and saw other troops that we became aware that something really unusual was going on. At the station, on tracks alongside of our train, we saw cars of other troops also being rushed to the Moroccan frontier.

Oujda

April 23rd

At Oujda, the first frontier town of Morocco, we realized what great military preparations were being made. It was only then that we learned of the precarious situation of the Protectorate of Morocco.

The men were tired from the two days' journey through Algeria. Now everybody had to work to unload the cars, and it did not take more than an hour for the legionnaires to remove everything, and to pile in order their material and arms. We then marched off through the town to the barracks that had been assigned to us.

The men, notwithstanding their fatigue, marched well and were admired by every one. All the officers and all the men of the garrison met the legionnaires with cheers and enthusiastic greetings.

During the day and evening men and officers both learned for the first time of what had been happening in Morocco for the past few months.

V

THE MENACE OF
ABD-EL-KRIM

OUJDA, AT NIGHT
April 23, 1925

TROUBLE had been expected for a long time
on the frontier of the Spanish Zone. While
the relations between the natives and the French
were excellent in the French Zone, there had been
trouble always in the Spanish Zone.

It can be ascribed chiefly to the warlike nature
of the Riffs, who inhabit the high mountains of
the Spanish Zone. These mountain tribes were always at war with one another, and always there were
chiefs appearing in the various tribes who wanted
to conquer the neighboring country.

Abd-el-Krim was one of these chieftains. By his
successes in guerrilla warfare against the Spanish
outposts he acquired prestige among the natives.
His forces augmented, he surrounded some Spanish
detachments and succeeded in taking away from
them arms and munitions and machine guns. By
these further successes he gained more and more

influence with the chiefs of the mountain tribes and finally in 1923 he captured a whole Spanish Army and became the great man of the Riff.

He released the prisoners only after heavy ransom had been paid. All the cannon and machine guns were captured, thousands of rifles, millions of cartridges, provisions and all the outfit of field telephone and field telegraph. He then conceived the idea of breaking into the French Protectorate, where the tribes had been living in harmony and peace for the past fifteen years.

The frontier tribes in the French Protectorate became aware of the danger approaching from the Riff. The news spread with great rapidity through the mountains. It is amazing to see how rapidly, without telephones or telegraph, only by runners who go from one village to another, from one mountain to another, from one tribe to another, the news is spread. Of course, these native tribes living on the frontier of the Spanish Zone in the French Protectorate knew about the success of Abd-el-Krim. They knew also how many men he had under arms and what forces the French had to protect them in case of attack.

During the winter of 1924, before starting his drive into the French Zone, Abd-el-Krim sent out emissaries to the frontier tribes living under the

French to warn them that they must come over and join him or be exterminated. He asked them, if they did not believe he had forces strong enough to do it, to send their own men into the Riff and see how many armed men were assembled on the frontier road to break into the Moroccan country.

People went there. They saw. They really saw many, many hundreds of armed men and a great display of munitions and armaments. They saw warriors ready at a signal to sweep everything before them. They came back to their villages. They told about it and, naturally, consternation overtook the tribes who lived on the frontier. Their chiefs would come to the officers commanding the French outposts. They would say to them:

"Friend, do you know of the danger? Do you know how many armed men are against you? What forces do you have? We are afraid. Will you be able to defend us? Our women are terrified. Our old men are saying that if you cannot protect us they do not know what will become of us. We shall all be killed. Everything will be ruined. Everything will be put under fire. What are you going to do? What measures are you taking?"

The officers in the outposts also knew the danger. But what could they do? Not only had the number of French troops in Morocco not been increased after the defeat of the Spanish armies, but through a desire not to appear militaristic the French forces in Morocco had been diminished year by year; and although these isolated officers, shut up in the outposts, had notified the High Command of the situation, the High Command could do nothing to help them. And for one reason or another, plausible or not, or for no reason at all, no men were sent to help the outposts.

Again and again the most friendly chieftains living around the posts would come and say:

"But the time is nigh! They are coming! They are coming! What are you going to do? What are we going to do? How will you help us? Where are your troops? Send only a few hundred men who will show themselves to our men and reassure the peasants that live and work on their land. If we are reassured, we will help the troops. Can't you send arms to us? We could defend ourselves if we had your help."

And then, one dark night and another, and finally almost every night, in some part of the northern frontier, a mile away from this post, or two miles away from that one, not being noticed by the small garrison, armed bands of fifty or sixty men would break in between the posts and set fire to the villages and houses and tents of the natives.

174

They would devastate everything. They would fire all that could be burned, take away the cattle, and sometimes kidnap women and children and take them into the mountains. Before an alarm could be sounded, before the outposts could fire the cannon or machine guns, before the natives themselves could take up arms, the brigands would fly away. And they could not be followed, even if there had been an armed force, because, on account of international treaties, no French armed men could pass the theoretical boundary established by treaties.

And the natives did not understand it. They did not ascribe our vacillation to submission to international laws, but to fear and weakness. No one in the world could have made them understand that brigands must be left unpunished because of a treaty made between different nations.

This submission, this civilized display of faith and integrity, could not be understood by men who knew no power other than force. And force was not shown.

After looting and brigandage had gone on unpunished, unchecked, for months, disturbances broke out in one part or another of the frontier. With all the personal amity in the world toward our officers, the natives had to decide. Everything was at stake

175

—their fortunes, their happiness, their homes, everything they had! Their honor also.

Many of the chiefs who decided to go over and join the Riffs even told our officers that they intended to do so. Some of them did not tell; but immediately before their involuntary desertion of the Sultan of Morocco under whose rule they were— just the day before, several of them invited our officers to their *kasbahs*. Our officers went unarmed, without escort. No harm befell them. The officers returned safely to the garrison. But the next morning they noticed a movement in the villages, an unusual going back and forth. Then following the trails and the mountain paths, long lines of men and women and children could be seen going to the north. Thousands of cattle herded by mounted and armed shepherds, were also being driven to the mountains.

A new migration started! A migration such as had not been seen for years and years—not since all these tribes had settled down to enjoy the peaceful cultivation of their land and the benefits of peace. Another migration! Another upheaval! All this was so familiar to the old men of the tribes, who expected nothing good to come of it. They were sad, they were loath to leave their homes to go into

176

the mountains. But still they went farther and farther into the mountains, and delivered themselves to leaders for whom they had no respect. They went to people whom they had known always to be cruel, to those who were really weaker than themselves.

But what could they do? They were made to believe, by the agents of Abd-el-Krim, that nothing would be taken away from them. That, on the contrary, even land would be given to them for their cattle to graze upon, that they would be established in a country where they could build their homes temporarily until Abd-el-Krim conquered the Sultan of Morocco. Then he promised these chiefs that he would give back to them even more land than they formerly owned.

Did they believe it? Who knows and who will ever know? But still they went. They marched on. It was not until they reached the Riff that they learned what fate had in store for them. All their cattle, their belongings, their property, their women and children and their old men—those who could not mount a horse or who could not walk—were sent into the interior of the country. They were held as hostages for the men, who were immediately surrounded by regular forces of the tribes of the Riff and made to fight against their Moroccan brothers

177

and the French who had protected them. To all
these men, who until yesterday were peaceful peasants, inflammatory words were spoken, their belliger-
ent instincts were aroused. They were made to
obey and to fight, and so they fought.

First the advance outposts, then those in the
rear were surrounded by the Riffians. All the outposts on the north bank of the Ouergha River were
surrounded and completely isolated from the rest
of the world. And the great siege was on. The
Riffians dug trenches around these posts in order to
prevent succor from reaching them. Then, and
only then, reënforcements were sent and soldiers
were rushed from every part of Morocco and Algeria to the rescue of the besieged men.

TAOURIRT
April 24th

There are several ways in which a battalion can
travel coming from Algeria to Morocco. If there
is no need for haste, the legionnaires make the
journey on foot. If it is urgent, they are transported by the narrow-gauge railway or by motor
lorries, carrying with them only their rifles, machine guns and munitions, all the animals walking
on the road and joining them afterwards. But in
a great emergency everything—the baggage and
178

all the mules and horses—travels by railway. This was the way we came.

After the two days' journey through Algeria with its richly clad fields and hills, with its gardens and vineyards, this first day of crossing Morocco was monotonous. Here was bare country, scarcely a tree in sight. Bare mountains, hills and rocks were on both sides of the road, and far to the north there were other mountains, higher, still farther away—the mountains of the Riff.

EN ROUTE FROM TAZA TO FEZ
April 25th

The battalion reached Taza and walked through the new European quarter of the city. A camp was formed on the outskirts of the town and the population brought all kinds of foodstuffs for the legionnaires. After the evening meal the men had authorization to go to town. At midnight all the officers were called to the commander's tent to receive instructions for the further march of the troops. They were informed that the battalion was to march off before daybreak. Roll call was ordered immediately in all the tents, and many men were found to be missing. Then in the darkness of the night and in the silence of this Moroccan town, the Legion bugle sounded *Rassemblement Générale.* Every battalion

179

has its own call, and on hearing it both men and officers are obliged to gather in their tents. Half an hour after the bugle had sounded, the roll call was again taken and every man was present.

At three o'clock in the morning, fires were started at the camp and coffee was prepared for the men. At four o'clock, the battalion was on the march. Notwithstanding that it was the month of April, there was great heat—distressing heat—and dust on the road. Men making their first march after days in railway carriages found it hard to cover the ground. It is always difficult, this first march, when men are not accustomed to the strain. Many were falling by the side of the road, but they had to go on. They had to reach the halting place, because Morocco was no longer a peaceful country where people traveled safely and without taking precaution.

Men always have in themselves much more energy and much more capacity than is shown at first sight. The question for a leader is, by what means he can bring out all the vitality that they possess and transform it from a static into a dynamic state. Men in their everyday life use only a small proportion of their capability, their talents, and everything that is given to them by nature and God, until some imperative necessity calls it forth.

180

A legionnaire, who has tried so many things before coming to the Legion, and who as a legionnaire is required to do so many different things even in his regular routine, expands much more than the ordinary man in civil life. But in a campaign still more forces are required. In a campaign, a man has to give all he has in him. It is only a question of how to get it out, of how to set in motion these energies and resources and to make them fit into a certain plan.

In these first days of marching, if the men were left by themselves on the road with no one to command them, they would think that already they had given all the strength, all the energy they possessed. Those who are responsible for the men must know how to bring forth all this latent energy.

How often I have seen men dropping by the side of the road! I think of one who could be taken perhaps as an example of physical exhaustion. The man was lying beside the road. With both hands he had torn open his shirt. His eyes were rolled up and his mouth was quivering, and he was groaning: "Jesus, Marie, Jesus, Marie!" An officer stopped beside him. What was to be done? There were no carts, no wagons following. The mules were packed—nothing more could be put on them. There was no one to carry him. He must not remain there,

181

yet the officer saw that he could not go on. The only thing he could do was to put him on his own horse. He whispered in the ear of this almost fainting man: "I give you my horse. Come—ride it."

The man opened wide his eyes, and the look on his face, that just a moment before had been an expression of extreme agony and exhaustion, immediately became strong and calm. He looked at the officer. He stood up. He said, "I . . . I on a horse . . . before all the men who march? I can go on." And he went.

Many times when an entire company seemed to be unable to endure any more fatigue, and the men with the great weight of the packs on their shoulders were just an assembly of pitiful creatures, the company would be stopped, and a few minutes' rest given. Then the command would come: "*Sacs au dos,*" "*Arme sur l'epaule droite.*" With the buglers sounding "The March of the Legion" . . . one-two . . . one-two . . . one-two . . . the company would go on, and every man, who, five minutes before, could not even drag along, would fall in rank and march as if he had been instilled with new energy.

Other times, the commanding officers, seeing the men absolutely worn out, would go alongside and give them a word of encouragement, or make some remark that would show real human pity. It would change the morale immediately. Some would start singing here and be followed by others there. From one section to another waves of energy would emanate, inspired by the songs, and wonderful and mysterious currents of vital force would sweep through the men.

How many hard marches have been performed by the Legion in various parts of the world during the last hundred years—Indo-China . . . Madagascar . . . Italy . . . Algeria . . . Mexico . . . Tunis. They have been bathed by the sun of two hemispheres. They have been covered by the dust of the roads of the whole world, the soldiers of the Legion.

A hardship which is overcome, an effort which has found its issue in action, latent energies which are called out and sent into a definite stream, a deed accomplished—these are always beneficial to an individual, and always purifying.

The outsider viewing a performance can seldom get an idea of the whole play. The separate parts may bear the features of the whole. Only those who through suffering and great love have acquired harmony in their own hearts can discover in the Part the great harmonious features of the Whole.

In the evening when one saw the men finally approaching a fortress where they were to stop, or an advance camp that was to be their halting place, or just a spot in the wilderness which was designated as their camp, one could almost see new energy flow into the hearts of the men. They would become cheerful. Their eyes would glow, and having reached the goal they were ready to march on if it were necessary.

Always about half an hour before reaching their destination, picked men from every unit, men known for their strength and marching ability, would start off with the commanding officer at a rapid pace toward the spot where the camp had to be made. There they would outline on the ground the plan of the camp, and every unit would know its place when it arrived. The liaison men would call out their respective units, which already had their places assigned to them.

Every company would march in single file along the line of the front that it had to defend. They would cover all the space assigned to them, standing equal distances apart. Then every sixth man would lift up his bayonet, and these bayonets, evenly aligned, would show where the tents were to be placed. And just as the bayonets were aligned, the tents of the men were aligned, equal distances apart,

184

forming as a whole a picture of order and precision. These camps, built and shaped up so regularly, looked like an ancient engraving.

Fᴇᴢ
April 30th

After several days of heavy marching we stopped for a two days' rest. In the morning after a calm night of sleep the legionnaires went to bathe and to wash their clothes in the creek near by. Perfect serenity reigned in the camp. The smoke from the kitchen fires was rising into the sky. · The men at the creek were playing, singing, splashing water on one another. Those who remained in the camp were writing letters. The noncommissioned officers were sitting on empty wine cases in the tent of the canteen. Perfect relaxation . . . peace. . . . Everyone had forgotten the fatigue of the last days, forgotten the dangers passed, and those awaiting them in the future. The legionnaire changes his mood quickly—almost too quickly.

But what was the dust that appeared on the road? What was the noise? The roaring of a motor. At full speed a motorcycle was approaching. A messenger! An order, to break camp at once! More clouds of dust and more noise on the road.

185

Nearer and nearer. One motor lorry after another, in an uninterrupted procession they came. The buglers sounded *Rassemblement Générale*. They sounded it again. And then they sounded *Au Pas Gymnastique*. All the men at the creek, some of them completely naked—many only half dressed—carrying their clothes in their hands—came rushing to their tents. Hurriedly they packed their wet clothes. In a few minutes everybody was dressed and armed. The men quickly broke camp, and we were ready to start. Twenty or thirty men were piled into each lorry, which at once started back along the road. With what joy the legionnaires climbed into the cars!

Our battalion was to be rushed into Fez. Men were ordered to have their rifles in their hands. Why? While on the road rumors spread. Whether these rumors came from the lorry drivers or started among the men themselves, it is difficult to say. But it was rumored that Fez was besieged by enemy troops, and some even said that the city had been taken by the Riffians.

On and on we went, and the bare country that we crossed gradually transformed itself as we approached the ancient city into a region where beautifully cultivated stretches of land were seen. Once more we saw the green of trees and gardens, so grati-

186

fying to the eyes after many days of sun and dust.

The outskirts of Fez were in sight. The natives came out of their mud houses and waved cheerful greetings. Children appeared, looking curiously over the fences of the gardens. The legionnaires were puzzled! Where were the stricken faces of a population in the midst of war? Nearer and nearer came the old walls of the city. And then at the gates that led into the heart of the ancient city men and women were standing, cheering the men and shouting.

But where was war? Where in this peaceful city were the signs of war? The battalion passed the old city and turned to the new quarters of the European town near which all the troops of the garrison of Fez were quartered.

The camp was laid out in a most orderly way. All the alleys and the lanes and the roads were lined with splendid trees. The trucks brought the legionnaires into the midst of the camp. Here all the soldiers—cavalry and artillery, the Moroccan and Algerian sharpshooters and the Senegalese—all were there to greet the new arrivals.

We expected to stay here for at least a few days to enjoy life in a city that we had not seen for such

187

a long time. The legionnaires were to have a day free for themselves.

Our arrival coincided with an annual Legion celebration which was fêted by all the four regiments of the French Foreign Legion, the anniversary of Camerone.

On the 30th of April in 1863, the Third Company of the Foreign Legion, sixty-two of them, legionnaires and sergeants, struggled for more than ten hours in the Legion's farm of Camerone in Mexico against two thousand Mexicans. On the evening of that day three hundred of the men who had assailed them were killed and were lying around the farm. The company was reduced to one corporal and two legionnaires. Finally they were taken by the enemy, but were given full military honors. Since that time this anniversary has been celebrated by all the Legion, the names of the men and the officers who fell on that occasion being recalled before the assembled units of the Legion, wherever these units find themselves. And the reminder of this splendid episode of its history, coming as it did on the eve of a great struggle, evoked in the Legion a spirit of intense pride and a determination to outdo itself in the forthcoming encounter.

Orders came to march early in the morning.

SOUK EL ARBA DE TISSA
May 1st

The farther we went, the more troops we began to meet on the road: Moroccan Sharpshooters, platoons of Moroccan Spahis, and, riding alongside the road there were Moroccan partisans, half cavalry, half infantry, composed of peasants from the districts of Fez and Meknes, who had been armed by their chiefs and were being led by them to battle. Not only the tribes who were directly menaced were coming, but those who lived hundreds of miles away from the front had taken up arms to march toward the Ouergha river. We passed convoys of food and munitions on their way to the bases established near the front where the fighting troops would find everything they required. Mountain artillery was following the trail alongside the road raising up clouds of dust. The day was hot. Both men and animals were struggling along with difficulty. Ahead of us marched a battalion of Colonial troops. The men were young, unused to the road, to the African sun, and to the dust and the blinding light.

The legionnaires marched gayly and swiftly singing songs, light-hearted and unconcerned. All the white troops in Morocco are obliged to wear cork helmets to protect them from the sun. The legionnaire almost never wears a helmet: he likes to coquette

189

with danger. We also had helmets, but had left them in our stores in Algeria, in the desert. Being with other troops, our men like to look their best. The songs they had been singing in half voice resounded now louder and more cheerful when we marched with the others.

For the first time all the detachments formed one camp and our battalion became a part of the "Column of the Upper Ouergha" which had to operate in the zone of the Haut Leben and the Oued Amzez. We were to protect Fez and to serve as a barrier cutting off Abd-el-Krim's approach to that city. We arrived at the halting place early in the evening, a few hours before sunset. As far as the eye could reach one could see a town of tents built up instantly on a place where just a few moments before there was no sign of human life.

The camp formed a square, all four sides of which were guarded by infantry. The artillery was placed parallel to the infantry and the cannons were pointed toward the mountains ready to fire in case of attack. In the center of the camp the cavalry was placed alongside the artillery. The convoy of mules was placed behind the cavalry. Then the merchants who followed the detachment installed their goods under large canvas tents. This place reminded one of a
190

village fair; here one could buy anything one wished to eat or to drink. Jews, Greeks, Algerians, Spaniards and Arabs from the coast gathered here to trade with the soldiers. There were also native acrobats, dancers and story-tellers, around whom the Moroccan troops gathered during the time of rest. After dark, acetylene lamps were lighted in the stores. A strange, ephemeral town it was. Then, when the bugle sounded taps, all these lights went out and darkness enveloped the *groupe mobile*.

AIN AICHA
May 3rd

In the morning we started for Ain-Aicha, the base of our future combats, which was already surrounded by the Riffians. We marched now in fighting formation, every unit being assigned to occupy a certain place in the detachment. The farther we went the more abrupt the country became.

We had to go over the high peaks of mountains. We passed through a few villages abandoned by their inhabitants. These villages looked much larger than those seen before in the Middle Atlas. And also the country in the valleys between the mountains was much richer than in other parts of Morocco. There were many rivers and creeks flowing from the high mountains in uninterrupted streams. In the fields the corn was already high, but in many places there were patches of ground where the crops had been burned by mischievous hands. In spite of our nearness to the enemy, we reached our objective without an encounter.

Ain Aicha was also a town that had sprouted over night. The ammunition and food were stored up in wooden barracks. The place for our detachment had been designated by the commander of the base, and each unit went to the line it had to occupy for the night. Facing the mountains where the outposts were, every unit in the camp was placed in the same formation that they would take the next day when going to the front.

Before sunset all the officers assembled at the tent of the commander of the detachment, then all went to a hill overlooking the camp, from which one could see across the valley to the mountains—a succession of high peaks—on which were our outposts. They could be detected with a field glass, and some of them, the nearer ones, could be seen with the naked eye. Each unit, in coördination with the others, was assigned to its task.

Then the captains of the different battalions took all the noncommissioned officers to the same hill, and the maneuver first of the whole detachment, then of every battalion, and finally of each company of the battalion was explained to all these officers in order that they might have a definite idea of what they were expected to do with their respective units. Not only the sergeants, but even all the corporals of the Legion were taken to see the country and explanations were made to them of the maneuver.

It has always been a custom in the Legion to explain every action to every sergeant and corporal of a unit so that if an officer is killed a sergeant can take his place. If a sergeant is killed, a corporal can take his place. And if the corporals are killed there are old soldiers who are designated to take their places. Designations of replacement are always made before a battle, and, therefore, there is never any confusion in the ranks of these disciplined units.

VI

RELEASING BESIEGED OUTPOSTS

At Night, after the Battle of Taounat
May 4, 1925

THE *groupe mobile* started before daybreak. It moved slowly and in good order to take up the positions from which it was to advance toward the mountains. Our battalion was in the advance guard. The Legion had the honor of raising the blockade of the first outposts which were surrounded by the Riffians.

Everything was quiet. There was no sound or sign of the enemy. No information had come as to the number of Riffians that we would have to meet. One of the posts, the central one of the group which we had to rescue, signaled by flashlight all during last night that they were being heavily pressed by the enemy, that they were still holding out, in spite of their exhaustion, and that for the last forty-eight hours they had not had a drop of water to drink. With this news we started into the mountains.

Thousands of men ready to start into battle were lying flat on the ground, hidden under the high golden corn. Then the bugle sounded *"En avant!"* The men jumped to their feet. The movement began in the prescribed formation. While the advance guard descended into the valley, the cavalry topped the hills to protect the advancing infantry.

Our first objective was a deep creek that cut the valley in two. After crossing the creek and advancing farther we received the first shots of the enemy. These bullets, whistling about our ears, were the first sign of the coming battle. After this everything moved very rapidly. We were in the midst of fighting. Shots were coming from all directions from groups of the enemy, hidden among the rocks a short distance away.

The troops fought their way upward. Already we had men wounded and killed, and when we approached the first hill that led to the higher range where the posts were, we were met with a heavy rain of bullets.

While the Legion advanced rapidly, all the *groupe mobile*, the thousands of men and the numerous convoys of animals moved on slowly. Then we received an order to stop, taking cover in whatever place we could find, to stand there as a wall, to protect the entire *groupe* in case the enemy took the

195

offensive. At that moment the main forces were attacked in the rear by a great number of Riffians who descended upon it. The enemy had already installed machine guns on the plateau and began rapid fire on our men.

At a signal squadrons of Moroccan and Algerian cavalry, together with the Moroccan volunteers rushed on the enemy, rapidly outflanking them, and driving them away from the position they occupied behind our troops.

Hours passed and we were still holding our positions. The enemy did not attack, but hidden among the rocks two or three snipers, aiming with great precision, brought down many of our men.

With my liaison men, the stretcher bearers, and some officers I installed myself in an abandoned *kasbah*. It was in the center of my unit, and I could command my men from there. We set up our machine guns, holding under our fire the slope of the mountain with its terraces of fenced gardens and houses.

Meanwhile many of our men fell wounded, and soon the *kasbah* was full of men with shattered legs and arms, with wounds in the chest, the stomach or head. Our first-aid men and the stretcher bearers risked their lives many times to bring in their maimed

196

comrades. The spirit of abnegation and self-sacrifice suddenly flowered. There was absolute defiance of death.

The Legion was eager to go forward. We knew by experience that the longer we waited the more difficult it would be to attain our objective. It was already far into the afternoon.

A battalion of Moroccan sharpshooters was immediately behind us. On our right flank there was quick firing. We were informed that an armored car on our right had been surrounded by Riffians. A section started to help it out, but could not get close to the car. It already lacked munitions.

The young lieutenant who commanded the section decided to get munitions from the armored car. But there were forty yards of ground to cover under very heavy fire.

Instead of ordering his men to go and fetch cases of munitions he went himself.

I see him step from his cover with a stick in his hand and walk across the field. We hold our breath, expecting him to fall at any moment. But he reaches the armored car safely, and taking two cases of munitions in his hands returns to his group.

Only then he asks for volunteers to go and bring more munitions. Ten men crawl on all fours to cover the distance. Six of them arrive. Immedi-

197

ately four more men start across the field, and with
the wounded on their backs they crawl back within
the lines.

While we stop there, facing the mountain, the
enemy becomes more and more daring. They inter-
pret our halting as hesitation or weakness. We see
the Riffians jumping from one rock to another, with
yells and shouts appearing within two hundred yards
of us. They disappear in the deep ravines only to
appear again on the right or on the left.

Finally in the distance we heard the bugle sound
"Charge!" That was what we had been waiting for.
With fixed bayonets, the legionnaires, disciplined in
battle as in exercise or maneuvers, did not rush forward at the very start. They went on slowly, steadily, unwaveringly, and as far as the eye could reach
we saw our men going on and on, climbing the rocks,
falling down, climbing again, all of them in order.

The whole line was advancing steadily, and there
was no stop until all obstacles had been overcome.

We passed a village on our right. It was necessary to occupy it in order to protect our flank.
It was large—more a town than a village,—with
narrow streets, high walls and arched gates, all of
them closed.

We opened fire on it. Then we entered with
198

bayonets fixed, and opening one gate after another we fired into the courtyards. The legionnaires shouted and yelled, and although excited did not depart from the usual discipline and obeyed all orders.

The place was searched and not a soul was found, but there were a lot of sheep and fowl wandering about the courtyards. Finding this live stock greatly cheered the legionnaires, who forgot even that they were in danger. Before leaving the village they stored up chickens in their haversacks and some of them tied sheep to their belts, for the evening meal.

Assured now that our flank was safe from attack we advanced rapidly and attained Taounat, the post which had been besieged by the Riffians and cut off from the world for the past two weeks.

There was a moment of great emotion. The besieged men advanced toward their liberators with tears in their eyes. All were greeting one another. The battalion received congratulations from all the chiefs.

The recompense and satisfaction were great. The fatigue and the danger were at once forgotten. The legionnaires were proud of the accomplished work.

This was the first post to be wrenched from the

199

clutches of Abd-el-Krim, who had held Taounat as the pivot of his offensive against Fez.

The posts were released and we camped around the fortifications. In the evening the mountains were alive with camp fires started to prepare food for the troops. Across the mountains to the north there were the other camp fires—those of the enemy.

The men we had come to save told us many tales of privation, of hardships, of great tension which all of them had suffered during the siege.

They had lacked food and especially water. Aeroplanes had been sent to furnish water by throwing down blocks of ice, but sometimes these blocks would drop inside the post and sometimes a few yards outside of the post, among the Riffians. The area of the outpost is small and the aeroplanes, flying high and rapidly, had difficulty in dropping the ice into the post.

The garrison of Taounat was composed chiefly of Moroccan troops. In the central post there were several chiefs of frontier tribes, who, notwithstanding the threats of Abd-el-Krim, did not go into the Riffian mountains, but took refuge in the outpost hoping for a better future.

This was the first of a series of battles that we had to fight in order to raise the blockade. Our losses were heavy. One captain in our battalion was wounded, also two lieutenants, four sergeants, and many corporals and men.

We did not stay long at Taounat. There was no time to lose. We had to go on and free other posts. Men were waiting for us. More than seventy posts must be freed from the grip of the Riffians.

KASBAH DES OULED BOU SOLTANE
May 5th

We were charged with a mission to go westward in the direction of the outposts we were to release. We had to find out whether the country was clear of Riffians, and if not, to find out what their strength was. Two squadrons of Moroccan cavalry went with us, as well as a battery of 65's. We were to keep in touch with the *groupe mobile*, which was ready to follow us if we should be engaged heavily by the enemy. The country seemed clear. Not a shot was fired at us.

All the *groupe mobile* joined us later in the day and we camped on the left bank of the Ouergha River, facing another group of posts that we have to release to-morrow.

During the entire night our camp was attacked. We could distinguish very clearly machine guns firing upon us from one of the peaks which we were facing.

GARA DES MEZZIAT
May 8th

The Legion is in the right flank guard, and one of the Moroccan sharpshooter battalions is an advance guard. Placing ourselves at the right of the ridges of mountains, we are protecting the march of the Moroccan battalion whose mission is to liberate Bab Ouender, standing high upon the mountain —a post that we can see with the naked eye.

The Moroccan battalion went alone. It had nothing to fear because the mountain was bare and we could hold under fire any forces of the enemy that might come from the right.

We saw them reach the top of the mountain. We saw them walk inside of the barbed wire around the post. We expected them to come back at once, together with the garrison of the outpost and the mules packed with all that could be carried away. They were to blow up the post just before leaving, as we did not intend to keep it.

Hours passed! There was no sign of the returning troops. It was already late in the afternoon. We had been all day under the terrible heat of the sun with no cover—with almost no food. Food had

202

not been taken because we had expected to return very soon to the camp. We waited. No orders arrived. About five o'clock, when the sun was already behind the high ridge of the mountains, we received an order to retreat from the position we occupied.

The Moroccan battalion had finally signaled that it would stay at the post over night, on account of the mass of Riffians who had gathered to the north and cut off their retreat. All that day, we had heard intense firing coming from behind the mountains, although we could see nothing.

We had to retreat. Our battalion, from the right flank it had occupied during the day, passed into the rear, and now our mission was to defend the retreat of all the detachments—the retreat to camp.

The retreats in these regions were always much more costly than the advances. While the natives did not dare to meet us when we advanced, because of our superiority, as soon as we started to retreat, they would follow us closely, and always the losses would be much greater than in the movement forward.

We waited until all the troops of our detachment were already crossing the river. Then we made ready to start back. In the battalion there would be a company that would face the enemy while the rest of the three companies would go back. In a company there would be a section to hold the enemy under fire while the other sections retreated. And so to-day, gradually, company after company, section after section, group after group, the retreat was made, without haste or confusion.

At the moment when the last company was getting into motion we saw several pack mules coming down the mountains, followed closely by groups of men. We thought that perhaps, after all, the Moroccan battalion was coming back. Night was approaching. The legionnaires looked at one another. We knew that even if these on-coming groups were our own troops, they would not have time to cross the river before dark. And we—who had to protect the retreat—what would become of us? Coming within less than three hundred yards, they unmasked their intentions, firing one round after another upon us. Several legionnaires were wounded. Our machine guns opened a deadly fire. Many fell. Abandoning the pack mules, which advanced toward us, the Riffians took their wounded and rushed back. They had wanted, perhaps, to engage us in battle, and draw us into the mountains, but their ruse had not succeeded.

Again we began our retreat, sending out first the heavy material in order that it should not hinder our swift movement.

204

It was becoming more and more dangerous. When the enemy saw us retreating, they followed, with increased forces. Stopping the battalion to see whether or not the groups of men and mules were our friends had caused us to lose more than half an hour. When the first sections of the battalion were crossing the river, those who remained on the near side had to repel attacks of the enemy. Cold steel was used. The legionnaires fiercely counterattacked. Several bayonet charges kept the enemy in check. The other troops had retreated and most of them had reached the camp so that we were left almost alone to face the hordes of wild Riffians.

Fortunately a platoon of native cavalry came to our rescue. They had already crossed the river. These Spahis, one of the best of the crack cavalry troops that exist, are always ready to give a hand to the legionnaires, and in attack or retreat they always can be counted upon. We always help one another. Seeing us in trouble they recrossed the river and dashed against the enemy. The young lieutenant who commanded this platoon told us that he would remain there until we were all on the other side. Being mounted it would be easier for them to break away from the enemy.

We had to climb a steep hill to reach our camp. The Spahis followed us. Some of their horses,

205

wounded, were abandoned, and the men were carried on the saddles of their comrades. Soon there were many horses which had to carry a double burden. We had several wounded men also. Our officers alighted from their horses and placed the wounded across their saddles.

No sooner had we reached the camp of Gara des Mezziat than firing started from all sides. In the darkness that falls immediately after sunset in these southern countries we heard the shouts and yells of a great number of men very close to the earthworks that had been thrown up to protect the camp. Not yet recovered from the fighting in the retreat, we once more had to rush with our rifles, bayonets fixed, to the walls in order to repel the attack.

It was one of the fiercest attacks that had ever been made on a camp. The Riffians even brought up machine guns, and then, for the first time, we experienced hand grenades thrown into our camp.

The skirmish lasted more than an hour. It would stop for a second; we would hear groans and moans from the wounded enemy that lay before the walls; then shooting would start again. Finally it ceased. The wounded were carried away by the natives, but in the morning we saw dozens of their men dead on the field.

206

SAFSAFAT

May 14th

Reveille at two-thirty in the morning. A clear, a magnificent moon. Imagine the reveille of thousands of men who camp. They are still sleeping, tired from the fierce day of fighting. At the sound of the bugle they pull themselves together. They strike their tents. Two men in each section light fires to prepare coffee. By the light of these numerous fires one sees shadows moving. One hears the neighing of the horses, the pawing of their hoofs, the shouts of the sergeants, swearing in all the languages of the earth. The companies and battalions are assembling at the point indicated yesterday. Again we have to cross the river. Even in the places where the water is shallow it comes over one's knees. Day before yesterday we crossed the river four times. They are wet, our men. They shiver, they cough, they swear—but they march, nevertheless!

Once on the great white plain we take formation. In the bright light of the full moon one begins to distinguish the alignment of the units. This mass of armed men and packed animals! Everybody is being placed in order and one can distinguish now the advance guard . . . the flanks . . . and the rear guard is losing itself in the distance.

The bugle sounds "*En avant!*" The heads of the

battalions, of the squadrons, give signals for departure, and the march begins. The east becomes clearer, the sun is ready to come out for another day.

We are the advance guard. We have to go to protect the retreat—or, as we call it here in Morocco, the *decrochage* or "unhooking"—of the battalion of Moroccan sharpshooters. Besides, during the day we have to occupy a certain line in order to protect the revictualing of two other outposts.

All that day was extremely hard and painful. We did not enter camp until six o'clock in the evening. All day the men had nothing to eat except a cold bite. The officers were in the same condition. Arriving at the camp we had to pitch our tents and prepare food. The day had cost us one sergeant wounded, who was carried on my horse from the line of fire to an ambulance. This is the fourth wounded that I have carried across my saddle, and often my white horse is colored with the red of the blood of my men.

Here on the Ouergha River we are not facing the tribes of the Middle Atlas or Taza, but are against well-organized resistance which is conducted in a most orderly way.

The country here is very fertile. The fields are

208

cultivated, the hills and the plains are covered with the green of corn, plentiful and magnificent, and this year the crops could have given wealth to the country which had begun to flourish under French protection. But now the tribes, taken away, or induced to go away, by Abd-el-Krim, have abandoned everything. They are now encircling our outposts. We are obliged to trample down the fields of corn sometimes to burn the villages, and the tribes have to be persuaded with arms to enter into our lines.

AIN AICHA
May 17th

It is a day of rest. For the last fifteen days the men have not had even the possibility of washing their clothes, of sewing their torn garments. We left all our baggage in Taza, taking with us only the strictly necessary things. My two orderlies, one attending to the horse and the other helping around, touch me deeply with their delicate and affectionate attention. Never have I lacked water. Every day immediately after the tent is pitched and the camp installed, I have everything that is necessary for my comfort. Sometimes I wonder where they have managed to get the water for washing.

Yesterday, in front of our camp a brigand was

209

shot. He had been found in the camp. He killed two men with a knife while they were sleeping, and snatching their rifles, tried to escape, but he was caught. In the early morning he was taken to be shot. He was big and strong, clothed in only one dirty piece of woolen rag. While his grave was being dug, he was sitting near by looking unperturbed. From time to time he would look at the sky and would smile. Then, when the preparations were finished, he stood erect before the soldiers who aimed their rifles at him . . . and he fell down dead. My God! Life and death! What is it all about! I no longer know! I have such pity and love in my heart that I cannot hate. Yet I make war. . . . I make war because I believe that it is in the service of Good. Yet, good or evil—are not we all children of the same mother, which is Life?

The wounded legionnaires who were being cared for in the hospitals were eager to come back. Often I received letters from the men saying that their wounds were healed, and they were impatiently waiting to return. One of them, a sergeant, wrote to me:

"I am discharged from the hospital and they have given me three weeks in which to convalesce. I feel quite well now, and I permit myself to write to you to tell you that. I also thought that you would not refuse me my legitimate desire to come and take my place in the unit, to come and answer the call 'Present' and take part once more in the hard but glorious moments that you are living through. I have learned from the wounded legionnaires who come here of the outstanding conduct of the battalion. You can easily understand how painful it is for me to feel myself isolated from you all, and to remain in a purely contemplative rôle. I assure you that I am well, and I gain nothing by staying here. I permit myself, therefore, to ask you to use all your influence and authority to bring me back to the unit. I may say to you that there are others of us who are eagerly waiting to return. When we see the motor trucks starting for the front . . . we just want to jump on them to come and join you. We cannot stand it to be inactive at a time when all our comrades are suffering, and here we are not doing our duty. Please let me hope that soon I will join you, and I hope also that you will understand my desire."

What trying days they were—those days we had to spend on a bare plateau, burned dry by the summer sun. No shelter under which to hide one's head from the burning sky. This merciless heat weakens the bodies of the men. Except those who are on duty as sentries and those who are designated to perform other duties, all are sleeping, covering their faces with their kepi, their backs against the bare rocks of the mountain. They are tired, my dear men. Too much has been asked of them. . . .

The mules, their heads to the ground, standing packed all day, are also tired.

To-day we arrived early at the camp. Two posts were released without the loss of a single man.

I was asked to present to the colonel four of my men, who are to be decorated with the War Cross.

The legionnaire pays dearly for his glory.

May 20th

The night was calm. After midnight I went to visit the sentry posts, to make my regular nightly round.

What a strange meeting to-night with two of my sergeants! One was on duty, the other just sleepless. One a Hungarian, an intellectual, a follower of the Hungarian revolutionary leader, Bela-Kun. . . . The other an ex-German officer, a Monarchist.

Night unites men. The three of us were standing there around a heap of burning coals warming our hands. Nights are cool here.

The Hungarian, looking into the fire, spoke as if thinking aloud:

212

"And I am here. . . . Why? In this fighting unit. . . . I, who struggled for the brotherhood of man. . . . I always believed that the social order established by men was wrong. But since I am here I have learned much. I have come to the conclusion that merely by changing forms of government real progress cannot be obtained. Unless everybody is educated and becomes really free within himself, is capable of assuming responsibilities and obligations, no progress is possible.

"I think that revolutions always feed reaction. Instead of Good being established after a revolution, Evil arises. It stops the gradual and natural education of the people, and their baser instincts are aroused. Those of the revolutionists who assume power, in order to govern, are obliged to renounce their ideal. Why did I come to the Legion? Because here I feel free. My fighting nature finds expression. This rigid and severe discipline is a beneficial thing for those who before coming here could not discipline themselves—could not discipline others. I believe that this free organization of the Legion carries light with it, both to individuals and to countries. Are we not going into the wilderness bringing light with us? Then what better education for international life than the Legion, where people of all nationalities in the world live and work to-

213

gether? In one year more I shall finish my five years of service. Where will I go? Nowhere to go. . . . I shall remain here. . . ."

Darkness covered the camp. All was still around. A sentry coughed . . . another sighed loudly. . . . One could hear the snoring of the men in their tents. The Hungarian sergeant, after a long pause, said to me:

"Please pardon me, sir, for this effusion. It is stupid of me. I beg your pardon." He saluted and walked away.

I remained there with the ex-German officer, who had enlisted under the name of Dubail d'Argonne. He said it was his real name. But who cared here whether it was or not. . . . When the Hungarian sergeant went away, Dubail d'Argonne was about to follow him. I asked him to stay, for I felt that he wanted to speak. The talk of the other man had stirred him up. . . . There are hours when we feel that we can ask questions of those who do not ordinarily like to be questioned.

"You were an officer?" I asked.

"Yes," he said, "I was an officer . . . of the German Imperial Army. . . ."

"Why did you come here?"

"Because I hate republics. And a German republic is simply ridiculous. I loathe democracy.

214

It is contrary to human nature. . . . Democrats are false. They are all hypocrites. . . ."

"What do you mean? Are not all men equal before God and are not we all children of the same Father?"

He tried to hide his smile, his lips quivered, he looked at me almost with compassion.

"No, even in Heaven there is no equality . . . even in the kingdom of God. Even in the order of angels there are cherubims and seraphims, angels and archangels. Everything is hierarchical in life, and everywhere there is degree and rank. All live on different planes. But in the society which is called Democracy, chaos prevails instead of order. Those who should live on a high plane live on a lower one, and those who should never leave their lower plane, go up higher and look ridiculous. Is it perfect? No. Even in the cosmic life of the stars and planets, in the celestial spheres, there is leadership. The earth turns around the sun. The stars and planets all have their places . . . some obey, others follow. It is perfect. That is why you can calculate all this complex movement to a second. That is why you know everything which is to happen in coming years. There is perfect coördination in submission and leadership. . . ."

This philosophical monologue was suddenly inter-

215

rupted by several bullets whistling through the air close around our heads. We moved away from the dim light of the burning coals. Dubail d'Argonne said:

"With your permission, sir, I am going to make a round and see if everything is all right. These rascals watch us closely. Why do we not exterminate all of them? Just a cloud of gas. . . ."

He disappeared into the night.

The Legion. . . . The Legion. . . . Each man with his own thoughts . . . his own reasons for things. . . . Yet, in the Legion, there is Harmony and Order!

VII

FIGHTING IN THE RIVER

Bivouac near Moulay Ain Djenane
May 22, 1925

I CANNOT believe that I am still alive.

The two days of fighting have been terribly hard. Still more men killed and wounded! At one moment, encircled by the enemy, I thought I would not come through—neither I nor the handful of men who were with me.

At daybreak, at the edge of a high mountain, we stood, a group of officers, with maps of the country and with photographs, taken from airplanes, of the outposts that we had to release. It is the most difficult country we have ever been through. On the way to the outposts there are many villages, now abandoned, that were once thickly populated. There are three or four ridges we have to cross before reaching the higher outposts. When one studies the maps, even knowing that there will be much climbing and dropping, one cannot realize the difficulties these hills will present. The mountains are

217

so close to one another that, having attained one ridge, one must immediately descend perhaps six or seven hundred yards into the bottom of a ravine. There are not even trails to follow. And the movement has to be made under heavy fire from groups of natives posted here and there.

On this bright morning after sunrise we stood there and planned the attack we were to make, every unit learning what it had to do. The battalion assembled, company by company, the officers explaining the movement to their sergeants, corporals and men.

All the heavy material, the tents and all the baggage, remained in the camp under guard of troops that did not participate in the operation. We went without sacks, without a change of clothing, without blankets—only two haversacks across the shoulders, in one of which was food for the day and in the other hand grenades.

There is a certain spirit in which the Legion faces difficulties and goes forward to attack. I have seen men of other units in similar moments. They are thoughtful; calculating their chances, perhaps. They are just as brave as the legionnaires, yet there is not that whole-heartedness that we find among the men of our troops. There is even enthusiasm in the way they start to attack. One thought occupies

218

their mind: to reach the goal set for them on that day. To-morrow, after it has been accomplished, perhaps even the same evening, many of these men will be sad and tired. They will be swearing, complaining.

But in the morning, before the day's task, they are anxiously looking ahead, indicating one to another the different points they have to reach, expressing their opinions as how best to accomplish their objective. Being professional soldiers, many of them having had military training in their respective countries, it is always interesting to hear what they had to say. Many times I learned from them. . . .

There is always keen interest on their faces; they adjust their arms, examine their rifles, verify the contents of their haversacks, unwrap packages of cartridges in their pouches. The only thing that one might ask of them is not to be so rapid, so swift in their movements. Always it happens that the Legion is ahead of the rest of the troops, and while attacking no one can keep pace with them. It was the same even in the World War—in the great attack of May 9, 1915, when the Legion, in forty-seven minutes, swept over five lines of the German trenches. It was to be taken in two hours and a half, and when we signaled that all the lines were

219

in our hands, the High Command in the rear would not believe it.

But here, in this guerrilla warfare, when a swift movement could change immediately a situation, when the carrying out of a swift enterprise could help all the other units, there was liberty of movement for the Legion, and enthusiasm overwhelmed everyone. There was such communion of spirit between the men and the officers—the officers believing absolutely in the bravery of their men and the men believing utterly in the capacity of their officers.

Everyone understanding the movement to be made, there were no more detailed orders to be given, and at the bugle sound of one command or another, everyone knew exactly what to do. When the bugles sounded, *"En avant!"* one saw a wave of hundreds and hundreds of men with their rifles on their shoulders, their bayonets clanking at their belts, in perfect formation, group after group, section after section, company after company, sweeping away all obstacles before them.

The first post to be reached was the small outpost of Srima standing isolated, and dominated by a high mountain only five or six hundred yards away. Almost no resistance was offered us here. The movement was so rapid that the natives had scarcely seen

220

us start before they saw the men already on the other bank of the river, scrambling up out of it, then climbing the mountain, and arriving at the post.

But what a strange reception we had!

Usually the men besieged in an outpost would open the gates and, all exhausted and pale, would greet us, if they had the strength to do so. Other times when we would approach a post in ruins no French flag would be flying. It would be a sign that there was only death within. We would find the bodies of men who had been killed, stripped of their clothes. . . .

But here, although the flag was still flying, the gates of the post were closed and no one was outside. Pulling aside the barbed wire we smashed the gates, and dashing into the courtyard we saw four men and a sergeant standing and presenting arms. This was amazing. It did not seem real. One could not believe his own eyes. What did it mean? I went straight to the sergeant and commanded, "Rest arms," and said:

"What does this mean? Why didn't you come and open the gates? And why are you presenting arms in a moment like this? We must make haste. We have to take away everything that you have here on the mules that are following. And then we will have to blow up this post."

The sergeant, who belonged to the Algerian sharpshooter regiment, and who was Algerian himself, trembling, his face pale, said:

"I beg your pardon, sir, but I did not receive orders from my commanding officer to open the post to any one. I was put here with the order to defend it. I did defend it. You will find in the other courtyard fourteen men wounded and killed. Only four men and I remain. We have not eaten for the last three days, and we would have dropped dead if you had not come. So when reporting on my action you can say that I did not open the post to any one."

I told this man that his conduct had been superb, but that his zeal was out of place.

My men came in. Immediately all the munitions were carried from the outpost. But while we were standing in the courtyard and the battalion was surrounding the post, we heard terrific firing. The Riffians hoped to take advantage of any possible confusion after we reached the post. But our troops had taken position to repel the attack. We threw hand grenades into the ravines from which the natives were emerging. In half an hour it was finished. Two of my men were killed in the courtyard and a few wounded.

The flag was still flying when everything was ready to blow up the post. We lined up, as well as we could under the circumstances; the bugle sounded *"Garde à vous!"* and then *"Au drapeau."* All the men presented arms, and the flag was lowered.

Then the sergeant of the post approached me and in a low, emotional voice said:

"Please allow me to take it. It is *I* who want to take the flag and bring it back to the commanding officer of my regiment. Please let me take it."

His request was granted. This was the last I ever saw of that man, but his pale face with the coal-black, burning eyes I shall never forget. His devotion to duty thrilled me to the depths of my heart.

After having liberated Srima, orders came telling us that we were to go to the post of Bou Adel and await further instructions. We had already made great effort in climbing to this post and the men had not had a chance to rest. They had to pack and load all that was to be carried away. They had not eaten anything.

The command was given to the men to take formation and Bou Adel was indicated. In spite of their weariness and hunger, they swept on toward their new objective, descending abruptly to the valleys. We went through the villages that were on the way. Twice we had to cross deep and rapid creeks that traversed the country; and then started climbing another height.

The men did not feel that they were in the midst of real warfare. It is true that there was danger—there were dead and wounded. But the men looked upon it as a race, a game—it was a question of who would get there first.

In this spirit Bou Adel was reached. Exhausted men came up to us, and officers and soldiers stretched out their hands, embracing our soldiers.

An old captain, pale, with a long beard, a man with marks of great suffering on his face, had been in this post for the last three weeks and had seen many of his men killed and wounded. They had had no food and no water for many days. He embraced me. He looked at my men, tears in his eyes, and his sergeants and the men standing around him also had tears in their eyes.

They said, "Why, these men of yours! These wonderful men of yours! We just saw you in Srina, the other post—not an hour ago. Then we saw you start away. We were wondering what you would do next when we saw some of your men climbing our ridge of the mountain—and here you are. It must be a great satisfaction to command troops such as yours. They are magnificent!"

224

All the outposts communicated with the *groupe mobile* by signals. The post flashed a signal saying that the Legion was there. I asked for further orders. They came: "Leave that post and go to the mountain which is on your left, the mountain that is facing Sidi M'Hamed, the big central post of this region, which is now being evacuated by three battalions of the Moroccan sharpshooters. Place yourselves in an advantageous position on the crest and await further orders."

We left the outposts we had relieved and again swept rapidly toward the position that had been assigned to us. That day the men were full of gayety and spirit. Was it the perfect sunshine that bathed us? Was it the wonderful free air of the mountains sweeping over our faces? Was it the enchanting landscape, full of green and full of color? I do not know. But it was a spirit of strength, of energy, of desire to overcome all obstacles that might be offered.

We established ourselves on the summit. A runner came and delivered further orders. We were to remain there for the next few hours. Only then the men realized what an effort they had made and how tired they were. They opened their sacks and took out the bread for their cold meal. There were boxes of sardines and pieces of cold meat. In their flasks every one had coffee and water. It was a well-earned meal!

From the top of our mountain, observing Sidi M'Hamed being liberated by the Moroccan battalion, one could see hundreds of men and hundreds of mules that had been brought in order to carry back all the munitions. Three cannon were in this post. They could not be carried. There was no time. The only road that existed went through a region not in our hands. Therefore, the cannon were pulled out of the post and made useless. And then, pushed by a few men, the wheels of their carriage making two or three turns, the cannon were thrown over the edge of the precipice with a crashing sound, taking on their way rocks that went with them into the abyss.

The troops began to leave the post. On the left, on the trail, we saw files of men and pack mules descending to the river and taking a path leading to the camp which was about three miles away beyond the ridges of the mountains.

We wondered what would become of us—what part we were to take in this movement backward. It was not long before the order came.

"Being in the center of the disposition, you must act as rear guard. Keep an eye on the troops in their return movement. As soon as you see that the convoy and the last elements of the troops have crossed the river, then you will break away and join the camp."

The order sounded simple, but it was not so easy to carry out. We had served before as rear guard, where we had to carry on our shoulders the rest of the troops.

The post of Sidi M'Hamed was blown up. After the smoke of the powder disappeared we saw groups of men clad in white and gray burnouses roaming around the post. These groups increased in number as the minutes passed. I saw clearly that the retreat would be most difficult. Here we were left almost alone; we had to form our own flanks and our own rear guard. Our safety depended solely upon ourselves.

When the other troops were about to cross the river, I began to send all the mules and the wounded men back. The descent from this mountain was abrupt and precipitous and it would not be easy for the animals to reach the river. Further to lighten our burden I also sent away all the mules with the machine guns. I counted on the swiftness of my men, depending only on their rifles and the hand grenades to make our way through to the camp.

The natives in the mountains are much more shrewd and observant than we are, because they are

227

accustomed to their mountains. They know them perfectly through and through. They thought also that the troops would retreat caring not so much for the enemy they left behind as to get away as soon as possible.

But they miscalculated—these sagacious natives. As soon as I saw that groups of them were approaching nearer to us the squads of our men lying on the ground opened fire.

When I saw that my heavy material and the animals were reaching the river, I ordered the men to retreat. But no sooner did we leave the strategic points that we were occupying than we heard the enemy yelling and shouting quite near. They came on us from all sides.

I did not stop the movement. Our rear guard was formed of picked men, who were absolutely reliable and had proven themselves to be the most level-headed. These men with their bayonets fixed hid themselves among the trees of the olive grove that was on the mountain, and let the enemy again approach. Even when the Riffians were only within a few yards they waited silently. Not one of them fired a shot until the whistle blew. Then they rushed on the enemy with irresistible force. A few of the natives were caught, others fled, abandoning their wounded and dead.

A pursuit would be dangerous. The men wanted to go ahead but the bugle sounded "Halt, and retreat!" and the men, disciplined as always, came back.

The movement continued.

After a very difficult descent from the mountain, we came to a ravine and then climbed to the last ridge before reaching the river. The enemy might easily surround us at any moment.

Firing continued all the time. The enemy wanted to engage us in a fight that under the circumstances would be fatal for us. But again they miscalculated. We ignored the firing. Already we had in our ranks a few wounded men who were heavy and difficult to carry. First one would carry a man, then another would carry him, and then a third, so everybody had his share in the difficulty and fatigue.

We reached the last ridge. We had only to go down to the river and to cross it to be almost safe. But, to our misfortune, this mountain-top and all the slopes on the right and on the left were heavily timbered, and we could not see what was going on.

Our men, carrying the wounded on their backs, began the descent, and at once firing started. We were assaulted from the rear and both flanks. Half of my men—I could see them plainly—were already crossing the river. Not having received an order to stop they thought that we were proceeding with our retreat without great danger. But at this moment we were fired on from the front. We were surrounded. No movement could be made forward. I decided to call my men back.

Three runners were sent out. Only one reached the other side. One was killed and one was wounded. I saw my men crossing the river once more, under heavy fire. The old sergeants knew exactly what had happened to us. They led their men in a most judicious and perfect formation. They climbed again to the place where we were and the retreat with their help continued.

Just before the Riffians surrounded us I saw my orderly jump on my horse and gallop away. He crossed the river and disappeared into the mountains, heading toward the camp. I could not believe my eyes! Was he running away? How great was my surprise, when we had almost reached the river, to see this orderly, all red, sweat running down his face, his eyes almost out of his head, with two full haversacks on either side, rush up to me. He said, "The horse is safe in camp, and I have brought back two haversacks of hand grenades."

Finally, under heavy fire that grew more intense every moment, we reached the river. The first soldiers were already in the water, when we saw that together with us, on the right and on the left, as far as we could see, the Riffians were crossing, too. There we were in the river! All of us! It flowed rapidly and its cold waters reached the armpits of the men. The Riffians would reach the other bank first, for we had on our shoes and all our equipment while they were almost naked. Nothing remained for us to do but to stop and fight, standing there deep in the water.

"Fire!" was ordered. The men raised their rifles and groups on the left and on the right began aiming at the Riffians. They were amazed. They never thought that in a moment of such great danger we would stop and fight. They thought we would try to get away as quickly as possible, each one for himself, regardless of the wounded that had to be carried. Some of them started to go back. Many fell. Only a few replied to our fire. Their bullets whistled around our ears. I saw bubbles skipping along the surface of the water. Thanks to the courage and discipline of the men, we succeeded in getting across.

I looked back. The Riffians, recovering from their first surprise, were rushing madly after us. Enraged by our stand, they did not take even their usual precautions. They did not hide any more. They were a wild, fierce mob, shouting and yelling

231

and rushing on us, in order to stab us in the back before we could get to camp. I thought our last moment had come.

And then I heard the tat-a-tat-tat of the machine-guns above our heads. The officer who commanded the group of machine guns had installed them there in order to protect our retreat. This bit of strategy saved us.

When we came to the camp we carried all our wounded with us—not one of them was left behind. Only a few dead bodies, riddled with bullets, had been left.

On that day we considered that we had come from afar!

Never before had we been so near to death.

VIII

MOUNTAIN WARFARE

May 23, 1925

IN this terrible retreat I lost a sergeant, Kosloff, who was an ex-colonel of the Russian Army, one of the bravest men in our company, a man who bore with much stoicism the simple life in the Foreign Legion.

The first time I met him was during an inspection of the shoes of the legionnaires. I had just taken command of the company. All the men were lined up in their barracks, standing barefoot, and holding in their hands their shoes to show in what condition they were. It was then I saw Corporal Kosloff. The first lieutenant of the company pointed him out to me and said: "One of the best men in the company —a wonderful instructor, speaks French fluently, is very correct, and everybody has the greatest esteem for him. The Russians in the company address him as colonel."

I wondered who he was. The same evening I called Kosloff to my office and asked him if he was formerly an officer in the Russian Army.

"Yes," he said, "and saw twenty-five years' service."

I asked him why he did not ask to enter the platoon of noncommissioned officers. He said that he was contented with his present position. He told me that he was wounded several times during the Great War. He had a contusion on his head, and sometimes he had very bad hemorrhages, and, therefore, he thought he had better not take the responsibility. But when the company went to Morocco he was promoted to sergeant. He was the quietest man in the lot; never excited, always calm, he did not raise his voice when commanding, but his tone was convincing, and every one followed him without a murmur. His fellow-sergeants always had the greatest esteem for him.

The sergeant major came to me with Kosloff's personal papers and said:

"Poor man. He must have felt that it was his last day. This morning after reveille, before the company left for the attack, he came to me and handing me his wallet said: 'Keep it. I do not know what may happen. I would hate, if taken prisoner and killed by the Riffians, for them to learn that they had in their hands a former Russian colonel. In this wallet are all my documents—the certificate of my graduation from the military academy in

234

Russia and on a separate list all my services in the army are described. Keep it and after I am killed give it to my captain.' He felt, poor man, that this was the end."

"Who saw him in battle?" I asked.

"Three men reported his being wounded several times. The last wound he received was in his head— his brains were blown out. His section was climbing a steep mountain. They carried his body for some time, but the enemy followed close on their heels and they had to abandon it."

"Sure he was not alive?"

"No, he was dead. Every man in the section can testify to that. His body was carried for more than one hundred yards by two men who became absolutely exhausted, and one of them was shot in the leg, and had to be carried away by other men in the section."

On looking through his wallet I found the address of a woman to whom his papers were to be sent, and this letter addressed to me:

"This letter and my wallet will be delivered to you on the day which is to be the last for me in this world. One day or another it is bound to come. One who is born must die. Those who have a be-ginning must have an end. Coming from the earth we must return to the earth. Eleven years of fighting and the annihilation of every member of my family—first the War, then the Revolution—it is enough experience for one man to live through. I have a feeling that soon I will go, that the fatal day is near—it is approaching. But what does it matter? Everything lives in my heart and nobody can take it away from me.

"I beg to ask you to send my papers to the address which I am giving you. I would like them to be read by the person whom I loved and still love. . . . She chose another path. I could not follow her. I do not regret the path I have taken, and God help her to keep her path beautiful. Thank you for all —you understand all that I would say."

AIN LEUH
May 26th

To-day the Moroccan partisans found a few natives hidden in the cellars of the abandoned houses of the village we just passed through. They were for the most part old men and women, and a few children with horror-stricken eyes clung to the ragged garments of the aged. The partisans decided to take their prisoners to the colonel in command. While on the road these poor, miserable creatures were pushed along roughly. When the legionnaires saw that they were being badly used

236

I saw a dozen of them rush down the slope and push the partisans away from their prisoners.

"Brutes, brutes!" they shouted. "Leave these poor old folks alone! We'll take the prisoners to the colonel." I ordered the excited men to mind their own business, and at the same time reprimanded the chief of the Moroccan detachment for the misbehavior of his men, commanding him under pain of execution not to harm his prisoners. But to make sure, I sent two of my men to see that the prisoners were delivered safely at Headquarters.

OUED AMZEZ
May 27th

We are camping between big outposts with a blockhouse near by, and one can easily imagine the joy of the occupants of these fortifications in knowing we are near. Thousands of fires have been started in the camp. It seems like a great illuminated city, created as if by magic.

The officers have no tents. Neither have the men. Everyone has to sleep in the trenches that have been dug to protect us from bullets and from which, in case of attack, we are in a better position to defend ourselves.

Just before night bullets began to fall on one part of our camp. Those who had planned it had

not taken into account that the crest of the mountain, which seemed so far away, was in the hands
of the Riffians. They could aim perfectly at this
point, and do much damage. It was too late to
change the position of the camp. The only thing
to do was to take over the crest of the mountain.
One lieutenant offered to go and said that he could
find in his section volunteers to go with him. After a
day's heavy fighting it did not seem as if there could
be any enthusiasm left in the men, who for the last
eighteen hours had been passing from one danger
to another, from one critical position into another
without respite, and who now, back in their camp,
had not yet recuperated. But when the news spread
through the battalion that volunteers were being
asked for, there was scarcely a man who did not offer
to go.

Only twelve men were taken. Each man carried
with him two haversacks full of hand grenades, his
rifle and additional rounds of cartridges. The young
lieutenant also took a rifle and hand grenades. They
started off. They disappeared among the thick
bushes growing on the hill, vanishing quickly from
our sight. I would have liked so much to go with
them, to guide them, perhaps, if it were necessary!
But they did not need me. The young officer, who
two months before had had his first baptism of fire,

238

proved that he possessed the poise and judgment necessary to a man who is called upon to lead other men.

For several minutes the firing continued, regularly ... three ... four ... five ... shots every minute. Then we heard an explosion of hand grenades, and we knew that fighting was on. A little later it stopped. Within less than an hour the men all came back.

"How did you do it?" I asked him.

"It was very simple," he replied. "We took the Riffians by surprise. We were able to get near them without being seen. We were not more than fifteen yards away. There were about thirty or forty of them. We just jumped on them. We threw our hand grenades. They did not even have time to fire. Almost all of them fled. Some were wounded. A few wanted to resist, and hand-to-hand fighting took place. You see, I have lost my kepi. A man attacked me. I threw my rifle away, and grabbed him. He was not armed, either. We tumbled down and were on the edge of a precipice, and together we just rolled over the edge. He disappeared. But I caught hold of a dead tree and pulled myself up. And here I am safe and sound!"

This was the first time that a group of men went out separately from the unit. That same evening we decided it would be a good thing to create a *groupe franc* (a detachment of volunteers always ready to go in case of an emergency and perform some special duty), the officers in the battalion taking their turn in commanding this group.

Gara des Mezziat
May 28th

These last days have been most difficult. Hard and dangerous operations have taken place. Our battalion was always an advance guard when we went into the mountains. Returning to the camp we were usually the rear guard, covering by our fire the retreat of all the troops.

Torrid heat! Not one breath of air!

The men with their sacks on their backs, their rifles, cartridges, grenades and haversacks, really are reaching the limit of their endurance. The young officers, not used to African campaigning, who have just graduated from military academies in France, are suffering greatly. They are weakened by diarrhea, but they have the most indomitable spirit.

Safsafat
May 30th

I have not noted events for a few days. It was

240

impossible. And even now I can write only a few words. I am tired and sad. Twenty-seven dead bodies, enveloped in canvas sacks, are outside the campaign hospital, and the hospital itself is full of wounded. When one stops fighting one begins to feel the tragedy of all this. It is not our battalion that has suffered this time, but our turn will come. I do all I can in order to encourage the men—to cheer them up.

I hope that a few days of rest will be given us. It is absolutely necessary to shoe and clothe our men. They are in rags. Many have to march in their slippers. Their feet are swollen, but they say nothing, and patiently they wait for the day when their needs will be recognized by those in the rear, who seldom understand the needs of the men who are fighting. Our needs and dangers are almost unknown by those who have to deal only with reports. Time and time again I have signaled the necessity for new equipment and those in the rear would state facts, figures, undeniable, but without any meaning in the life that we have been called upon to live in the last two months. It is true that we were newly clad when we started away, and in ordinary times we would not need new equipment in such a short time. But when a unit has been fighting day and night, in mountains and on plains, in cold and in

heat, under pouring rain and under the blazing sun
—when such an effort has been made by a unit,
paper facts have no relation to reality.

June 2nd

We are resting at the camp to-day. The wind is
not so cold as it was and the sun is coming out. This
morning early my orderly came and brought me an
armload of wild flowers. He has covered the outside
of my tent with green branches, and inside he has
laid a carpet of green and flowers. My feet are
literally sinking into them.

These legionnaires, these rough men, these warriors, are so sensitive. Did they feel that I was
somewhat sad, or were they thirsty for beauty themselves? The fact is that without any orders on
my part, immediately after sunrise, they began to
arrange their camp. They have made lanes between
their tents. As there are no trees or green in the
camp, the legionnaires went to the foothills and
brought back trees and little palms that were growing there. These have been planted alongside the
lanes. Beds of flowers have been made. The camp
is completely transformed. It is wonderful to live
among the legionnaires—to command them. When
one understands them the leadership is easy.

242

Among the wounded noncommissioned officers one was an Italian, one of the newly promoted sergeants who joined the unit before we started on this campaign. I noticed him among the others. He was young, handsome, and has good manners—one felt that he must have good blood. He was wearing war decorations of his own country. I asked him what they were and when they had been conferred. He replied that he was an officer and that he went through the Great War. I told him that while I honored his decorations, there was a regulation in the Legion that no legionnaire could wear his former decorations. He would have to earn them in the Legion.

Once, when we were on a long march, I saw him, weary and tired, dragging along behind his section. I said to him:

"I should like better to see you at the head of your section and not behind—especially you, an ex-officer, with all your decorations."

But on the day that he was wounded I saw him at the head of his section, rushing forward, fearless of danger. Afterwards he wrote me a letter from the hospital saying:

"My foot is badly shattered, but I am recovering from the wound, and I hope to come back. The only thing I want to ask is—did you see me in battle? I would be so sad if you were left under the impression which you received when you saw me marching behind my section."

In this letter he also asked me to write to his father, a retired general, and president of one of the largest insurance companies in Italy; and he gave his real name and the address of his parents. He must have written home at the same time, because soon after, a letter came from his father asking me to tell him how his son had behaved. I answered that his behavior could be judged from the citation I had just presented to him.

Then I received another letter from his father, telling me that he himself had sent his boy into the Legion.

"Please do not think that he is a criminal or a murderer," he wrote. "He is not. He is young. He misbehaved himself. His passion for cards got the better of him and he did what a gentleman should not do. I paid his debts. Then I told him to join the Legion and if he did well for five years he could come back to his family. Now he is wounded. You write me that his conduct was brilliant. I am over-joyed, I am proud of him. He is once more my beloved Enrico. He will continue his service in the Legion and after the five years he will be once more accepted in the family."

IX

DISCIPLINE AND ENDURANCE

After the Battles of Sker and Astar

Bivouac at Taounat

June 6, 1925

THE release of the group of posts of Sker and Astar was conceived on a large scale.

Great forces of Riffians had gathered around these outposts, not only to prevent us from relieving them, but also to prevent our going farther and occupying the highest ridges. They had prepared themselves for a great resistance. For the first time during this period of the campaign we succeeded in bringing up our heavy artillery—75's, 85's, 105's—and there were even two cannon of 155's placed on the positions from which we were to start off. In order that the operation might be carried out with a minimum of losses, the flank guards were made stronger than ever. Our battalion was to protect the left flank of the advancing troops by occupying a crest of a high mountain, bare, with no vegetation, where once Astar had stood. Now it was in ruins.

245

All the garrison had been killed a few weeks before. We had to take over this bare mountain and re-occupy temporarily the deserted outpost. The aviation reconaissance had taken photographs of this region and we could see from them that trenches had been dug by the Riffians on the mountain. The taking of Astar would be impossible without the artillery to destroy the underground works of the enemy.

In Africa it is difficult to appreciate distances on account of the great thinness of the air. This mountaintop that we had to occupy seemed right before us all the time. Yet several steep ridges of mountains had to be crossed. In the deep valleys there were villages. We were to pass through one large village, and we were not at all sure that the enemy would not be there in ambush waiting for us.

Half an hour before we started the roar of big cannon was heard for the first time during our operations in the Riff. The ground was covered with the smoke of explosions. Artillery preparation began. First the ground that we had to go over immediately was shelled. Then, gradually, as we moved forward, the curtain of fire went before us and advanced simultaneously with us. It was calculated to a minute. All our movements were calculated in advance,

246

Artillery fire always gives confidence to the infantry, and when, finally, we started, our men were more animated than ever. Everything seemed easy under the cover of fire. Three battalions were advancing at the same time in one line—two battalions of the Moroccan sharpshooters and one battalion of the Legion. Everyone had his special piece of ground to cover and his assigned positions to take successively, according to the general plan. When, in the prescribed time, the Legion had passed all its successive objectives, we found that the other two battalions had not been advancing at the same pace, and we were all alone in the field, with no protection on the right or on the immediate left.

When we approached the foot of Astar, which we were to take, the artillery was hammering the top of it. We did not lose one man until then. The legionnaires were absolutely indefatigable. With Astar always in view, seeming so near that one could touch it with outstretched hands, there had been more than two hours of walking (and through what a country!) before we reached it. But once our men had set foot on the mountain they climbed it as easily as though they had just had two days of rest.

It was not until we were half-way up the mountain and everybody was panting and wet with sweat that fire was opened on us by groups of Riffians, placed here and there in caves dug in the side of the mountain.

Immediately I ordered my men to stop and take breath. Different groups were detailed to these caves, these strongholds of the enemy, by means of which they had planned to hold us in check. The legionnaires were impatient. There was no time to be lost. In a situation like this the quicker one moves the more advantageous is his position. Even though only a few elements of the unit would reach the objective, the enemy, crushed by the impetuosity and the rapidity of its assailants, would be demoralized.

It was with only a handful of men that I reached the top of the mountain, but even ahead of me there was one of our officers—a young, strong boy, a giant —who had advanced almost alone.

We saw the Riffians running away as rapidly as they could and we were in possession of the mountain. We were close to the abandoned post. We had gotten there with surprising ease. We could not believe that everything was over—that we were masters of the situation. Other groups and sections of the unit came up. The men brought with them a few prisoners taken in the caves. We hailed victory!

But we were isolated. There was no continuation

248

of our line on the flank, because the other units did not occupy in the specified time the assigned positions.

Immediately we began to organize ourselves in the ruined post—to put it in a defense position. The walls were still standing, although there were breaches in it here and there. Not far away, on the edge of a precipice, was a platform, which formerly had been connected with the outpost by a trench, through which one could walk to the platform unseen. Now the entrance from the post was filled up and there were twenty yards of bare ground to cover before we could enter the trench. We occupied the trench, facing the enemy, and on the platform where the cannon had once stood, a section of men with machine guns were placed.

We had not been in this outpost more than half an hour when we, especially the platform and the trench, were attacked heavily from all sides. We could not believe there was any one hiding, that any one could hide among these steep rocks. Yet on all sides we saw white and gray burnouses creeping cautiously from one stone to another.

Our men in the trenches and on the platform had to repel successive attacks from bands of Riffians. Several times the enemy came to the edge of the platform, only to be kicked off by our men. The firing was incessant. The Riffians came on us in a flood. We threw hand grenades into the midst of our assailants. With bayonets we threw them out of the trench, from off the platform. But they still came on. It lasted for more than an hour, this wild rush of the enemy, who had allowed us to occupy this position so easily.

The more vigorously we repulsed their attack the fiercer they became. Then came the moment when the legionnaires in the trench and on the platform had fired their last round of munition. Only a few grenades remained in their hands, and the cold steel of the bayonet.

Fortunately the attack now began to weaken. There were almost no losses among our men. The lieutenant who commanded the platform feared, however, that another attempt would be made to take his position, and there were no munitions. He decided to send a few volunteers to the post, in spite of the fact that more than twenty yards of bare ground had to be crossed under heavy fire.

On the post itself heavy attacks had also been made, simultaneously with those on the platform and trench. But, of course, we were in a more advantageous position. We were behind thick walls, and had placed machine guns on the bastions. Knowing that the defenders of the trench would soon be short of munitions, I gave orders to store up packages of cartridges and pile up cases of munitions for the machine guns. And I was ready to ask for volunteers to take these munitions to the men outside the post. I saw a place from which I thought the men could go out, with the munitions, into the trench. Just then I saw two men approaching—one very short, with a long gray beard, and the other a tall, thin legionnaire, the best singer in the company. They were smiling at each other. They were not walking toward the post, but were hopping about as if stepping on hot coals —like Fijian fire-walkers. The ground was almost shattered under their feet from the eruption of bullets. The short, long-bearded man had a pipe in the corner of his mouth. . . . The appearance of these two men would have been amusing if the situation had not been so critical. They entered the post. The short man was the most undisciplined legionnaire in the unit in peace times, but during the campaign he proved to be courageous and indefatigable. He stood there and saluted.

"We are rather short of munitions," he said. "After the hot bath we have given the Riffians, I don't think they will come again. Still we have to come for more food. There isn't one round of ammunition for the rifles, nor a band of cartridges for the machine guns."

I pointed to the stored-up munitions ready for them and said, "Here they are."

These two men, with two others who volunteered to go with them, walked out of the post absolutely unconcerned, taking no thought of the danger they would be in as soon as they left shelter. They calmly marched out with the heavy loads on their shoulders. All got safely into the trench, not one of them being hit, although as soon as they appeared in the open the unseen enemy began firing, and bullets were whistling and hissing and cracking all around them incessantly.

It is so much easier when one attacks an enemy that one can see, when one can measure the enemy's strength and the resistance that he can offer. But it is disconcerting to be under fire by an enemy that cannot be detected, and whose number is un-known.

There were a few wounded in the outpost already. They were taken care of and their wounds dressed. They were sheltered in the half-destroyed barracks. I went to see them. They were lying on the ground. A terrible smell came from one corner of the barrack. I started toward it and then felt that I was stepping on something soft. I reached

down to see what it was. It was the body of a
soldier, a sergeant who had remained there with
only three men after the rest had been killed and
who had finally flashed his last words: "*Le poste
est fichu!*" After that there had been silence. I
ordered a deep grave to be dug in the courtyard
in which to inter the body. We found that he must
have been tortured. His feet were charred and there
were bruises on his chest and back. . . .

We were cut off from the rest. We heard firing
at a distance on our left, and on our right and to the
northwest where the main operation was being carried on. We heard the explosions of shells, the
cracking of rifles, and we saw the spurts of flame
from the rapid fire of the guns.

What were they going to do with us next?

Then, with the approach of evening, we received
an order to remain in this post for the night, and
wait for further orders. But before night came
there was another outburst on the part of the enemy
to overcome us. We prevented their movement to
cut in two the main force of our advancing troops.
Again, with heavy losses, they were repulsed.

Night fell. Nobody thought of sleeping. I ordered the sentries doubled. I made the men rest
and try to sleep in order to be ready for any emergency. The night was extremely dark. There was

a mist lying over the mountains and in the valleys. It was impossible to see a yard ahead. The barbed wire that had surrounded the post had been torn down and the enemy could now approach to the very walls. But after their heavy losses during the day no attempt was made and the night passed in quiet.

The morning came, clear and bright, with a wonderful sunrise.

Soon orders arrived: "The operation of yesterday carried on in order to release the group of outposts of Sker has been successful. All the objectives have been attained. At seven o'clock in the morning the retreat will begin from the outposts to the camp. Keep strict watch to right and left. Enemies reported in your direction. When you see the blockhouse nearest to you blown up, prepare yourselves to leave the outpost within half an hour, and from flank guard you will become rear guard and protect our retreat."

Another retreat.

The nearest blockhouse was blown up. This was the signal to prepare ourselves to leave our position. As always, the heavy material was sent on ahead. The few wounded that we had were also sent away. The machine guns carried by the men followed. We had nothing to hinder us. We had only to slide down the mountain as quickly as possible, without losing a moment. We had to keep all our sentries until the last, until every one in the shattered outpost was ready to dash out. We tried to make our preparations for departure without being noticed by the enemy, which we knew was still around us. We emerged. We slid down the mountain in a cloud of dust. But no sooner had we left than white burnouses were coming from all sides—rushing upon us.

According to the orders given, the first element that reached the foot of the mountain was to climb to the first crest, in order to protect by its fire the retreat of the last elements. Then the last elements would pass them and stop in their turn, to protect by their fire the men who were leaving this first crest. Protected by the fire of the second group, the first element would then be able to retreat in order. So, successively, passing from one crest of the mountain to another, in perfect order and formation, one unit after another succeeded in getting away. And the enemy, hoping for a stampede, saw an organized retreat and suffered losses from the precise fire of the legionnaires.

Losing contact with our pursuers, we now entered a thickly wooded area. Divided into groups in touch with one another, we started to go through.

255

The woods were full of Riffians. The legionnaires did not discover them until they were only a few yards away. Without hesitation, without stopping, our men went forward, throwing hand grenades and completely demoralizing the enemy. The last element, with which I was marching, was attacked heavily from the right.

My orderly, who walked by my side carrying a hand grenade, said:

"This hand grenade is for us. For you and me. This time I think we will not get through. I know it. I am an old soldier. But we will not give them ourselves alive. I will throw the grenade and we shall be blown up—you and I."

The twenty or thirty men around me were just as calm as if they were on a maneuver. Every few minutes they stopped. They took advantage of every irregularity in the ground. Being good shots and having full presence of mind, they picked off the enemy one by one. This careful fire from men who were supposed to be running away demoralized the Riffians.

I saw one young legionnaire who had arrived with the last reënforcement. He was just as poised as an old legionnaire. Preparing to throw a grenade, he called out to me: "Here to the left! Hordes of them!" He threw his grenade, which fell with a loud explosion to the ground within twenty yards of us. At the same moment this young legionnaire was hit by several bullets. Bleeding from a wound in the neck, he still had time to throw another grenade before he fell. One of my men picked him up and putting him across his shoulders carried him away. My orderly was shot in the leg. Assisted by two men he was able to walk along.

Finally we were out of the grip of the enemy.

Already near to the camp, we stopped and re-formed our ranks. Many men were wounded, but they did not even notice the pain of their wounds. I have seen men shot in their hands, the blood running from them, their arms hanging limp, with the enthusiasm of battle still in their faces.

When the ranks were re-formed, we marched toward the camp. We were met by all the other troops, who came out to congratulate the men on their safe return. When I came to my tent and the orderly helped me to take off my equipment, all covered with dust and blood, he said to me:

"From now on I will always carry a grenade in my hand. If we continue with these retreats, to-day or to-morrow they will get us. . . . Once to-day— I do not know whether you saw me or not—I killed off two men. One of them, he recognized you to be an officer and he aimed at you. He aimed and he smiled—the devil. . . . I landed a bullet in his smiling face."

X

THE TRAGEDY OF MEDIOUNA

GARA DES MEZZIAT

June 9, 1925

AMONG the remaining outposts to be delivered was Mediouna. It was completely surrounded by the Riffians. It had no communication with the rest of the world. The men there were completely isolated and close to them the enemy had dug in in two lines of trenches, one facing the post and the other facing those who would come to deliver it.

We could see the white walls of Mediouna from the crest of the mountain where we camped, and where we had established our base of operations in that region. All the higher peaks that surrounded and overlooked the post were in the hands of the enemy. Two attempts had been made to deliver it, but the troops were under such heavy fire that, after losing many men, they had to retreat.

At present we did not have a large enough force to concentrate on that particular post. Other work had to be done. Other posts had to be relieved and

259

the country had to be defended from incursions of armed bands. Promised reënforcements had not arrived.

The troops that had been operating for several months were obliged also to build roads in order to carry supplies to the men in the field.

The position of Mediouna was daily becoming more and more tragic. And one day they signaled that if it were not possible to free them before the next day they could defend themselves no longer and would have to blow up the post and themselves with it.

June 11th

The Legion was eager to go.

The following plan was conceived: Forty or fifty men with two officers were to go there at night. They were to take with them only their rifles, rounds of ammunition and hand grenades. Also they were to carry everything necessary to blow up the post after it was released.

The commander of Mediouna had to be notified that he would be released on that night so that he could prepare to abandon the post and dismount the two cannon that were there. An aviator volunteered to fly over and throw down a note, advising the commander of the night's action.

The plan was accepted. Soon the note was written and the airplane went out. We saw it flying over the post and then it came back and the aviator assured us that the message had been delivered. All the officers of the battalion went to the edge of the mountain, from which they could clearly see the post. How we could release it without heavy losses and how the attack could best be made were the considerations with which we were concerned.

"At eleven o'clock the forty men and the two officers assigned will walk out of the camp as silently as possible and will work themselves toward the besieged outpost. A quarter of an hour afterward the entire battalion will go out in perfect quiet, cross the river and hide itself behind a ridge of the mountain in the neighborhood of the outpost, in order to protect the imprisoned men and their deliverers if they should be pursued after leaving the post."

The plan was to be kept secret. But when the forty men of the *groupe franc* were advised of the plan, of course they told their comrades and the whole battalion became excited.

Everybody knew and talked about the night attack. One of my men who served as a liaison—a young French boy, noted for his misconduct in garrison, yet who in a campaign proved himself to be

fearless—came to my tent. He handed me a money
order for five francs. He said:

"Please take this money order away from me. I
am a drunkard, and I cannot have this money in
my pocket and keep from spending it for drinks.
I know that to-night you will need me. Therefore
I don't want to have the possibility of obtaining
drinks."

This man showed the real spirit of all in the battalion. If he were not fit he would not have been
taken on this dangerous enterprise, from which there
would not be one chance in ten of his returning.
Yet deliberately he decided not to drink, in order to
be ready to accomplish his duty when the moment
of the night's attack came.

The muleteers, who have to remain in camp to
look after the animals, one by one came and offered
to go. The sergeant majors of the companies also
asked permission to go with the battalion.

Night fell rapidly. After the sun went down the
legionnaires went into their tents to sleep or to rest.
Nobody was to undress—all were to be ready to
start at a moment's notice. When the order came,
the forty men and two officers started off. Two
young lieutenants, not included in the order, went
with them. They had been classmates in the mili-
262

tary academy and they could not bear to leave one another.

Without a sound, without stirring up the camp, the battalion assembled to follow. The hundreds of men walked as silently as one man. It seemed as if every one was profoundly affected by the gravity of the situation—with the importance of the mission that they had to accomplish. On their silence depended the lives of those forty men and four officers and the success of the enterprise.

The battalion began to cross the river. In the night we could not find the ford, and we had to go through the cold waters which ran rapidly; in places it was over one's head. All wet, water dripping from our clothes, we assembled on the other bank. The moon was just coming up from behind the mountains. Heavy clouds were traveling high in the sky and these covered now and again the dim light of the moon. In the daytime we were well acquainted with the country, having crossed it on many occasions. But in this strange light of the moon everything seemed completely transformed; even the ridges of the mountains did not have the same shape that they had during the day. It was a mysterious, strange land through which we traveled.

In one long file, quietly and silently, we moved

263

along the edge of a mountain running in the direction of the post, keeping ourselves in the shadow.

More than an hour passed. We knew that we had to go through a field of corn. When we came to the field the first men stepped out from the shadow into the moonlight. It was difficult to go through this uneven, plowed ground, for we were still wet from crossing the river. The corn was shoulder high and the waving of the stalks gave the impression that some one was hidden there.

Suddenly a cry was heard—then a few rifle shots. Nobody knew from where they came. To this long file of men, traveling in the night, no orders could be given. It took a few minutes to check the line. Everything was quiet again. But through the silence we heard men groaning and moaning. A few of our men were wounded. Among them was a captain, a big, heavy man who was shot in his leg.

No one in sight. Who had fired? What was the cause of it? Nobody knew. There had been a moment of excitement. A soldier had seen something. He had fired a shot. It was followed by another. And perhaps the shots were all fired by our own men. No enemy could be found.

The task of the battalion became still harder, because the wounded men had to be carried. The silence was interrupted by their groans. We dared

264

not go nearer to the post on account of the noise made by the shooting. We decided to stop where we were. I looked at my watch. It was already two hours since we had left the river. The night was exceedingly cold and everybody shivered. Soon we heard firing start far away. We saw explosions of grenades flashing through the night. Perhaps these were our men who had gone on to deliver the post. We were expecting the development of the engagement of our men and we decided to stay where we were and wait for them to come back.

After this outburst of firing in the distance, everything was quiet again. We waited. Nobody was coming. We thought perhaps our group of men, who went to deliver the post, had retreated in another direction and would cross the river without us. We decided to go back. With great difficulty we again crossed, carrying our wounded with us, and established ourselves in a waiting position on the other bank.

The night was approaching its end. It became clearer and clearer. Dawn found us still waiting. Nobody came. Roll call was ordered. Was there any one missing in our battalion? All those who started were present with the exception of the two lieutenants—the ones who had joined their comrades without being ordered. . . .

265

The wounded were carried to the camp. Then a messenger arrived, ordering us to come back to the camp and saying that the enterprise had not succeeded—only three out of all that group of forty-four men who had left so gallantly the evening before had returned!

We started back to camp and while climbing the mountain we were met by the native cavalry. The commander said to me:

"We are going out in the field to see if we cannot find some of your men. Perhaps some of them, wounded, are lying on the ground—perhaps groups or isolated legionnaires are hiding in the mountains. But I fear everybody has been killed."

That was a tragic morning. We came to the camp. All the rest of the troops were out of their tents looking at us, the officers shaking our hands with sympathy.

And finally we saw the three men who had escaped. They were not yet in full possession of their faculties. They were dazed and shaken by the happenings of the night.

The expression on their faces was one of horror. The things that they had seen were reflected there. What had happened? One of them, a corporal, a big, powerful man, had all his equipment torn off. He said:

266

"It was simply awful. We approached the out-post in perfect silence. There was not a sign of the enemy. When we came to the last crest of the hill which was within three hundred yards of the post, so silent we were that we could see the sentries of the enemy who had entrenched themselves on this crest. They were unaware of our presence. We had time to pick off these sentries one by one.

"Then we decided to attack the trench, and by throwing hand grenades to destroy the enemy and dash ahead. We threw our grenades, explosions followed, and not waiting a minute we rushed for-ward. But no sooner had our grenades exploded than we heard all the mountain, all the surrounding country, awaken.

"Yells and shouts came from everywhere. We heard the mules braying. We heard the horses stamping their hoofs. The whole mountain came to life. And when we approached the post—near the barbed wire—we were met by hundreds of men in white burnouses who fired on us. Throwing grenades, firing shots, with our bayonets fixed, we attempted to break through the lines of the enemy to get to the post.

"We waited for the men inside to come out to help us. My lieutenant went into the post. I followed him. About ten of us succeeded in getting into it. We saw the lieutenant who commanded it. We were surrounded on all sides and there was no hope of getting away, but we thought that perhaps we could remain there until another force came to deliver us.

"The lieutenant in command said: 'No use. I have mined the post and it will blow up within a few minutes. We have to leave it, no matter what the cost.' There was nothing else to do. We started back. There was general firing going on. At one time I saw a lieutenant of ours already shot in the leg. He threw grenades right and left in a sort of madness. I saw another lieutenant, who with his bayonet was fighting desperately against dozens of men who wanted to take him alive. Even in the night you could see the shining of the steel, thrust from side to side, repelling one man after another. Many of our men had thrown the last grenade they had. They had fired their last shot and cold steel was used.

"The enemy was everywhere, and more and more were coming from the mountain. The fighting was most desperate and fierce. I could see that not one of our men had given himself up alive. I saw a group of eight or ten of our men fighting with knives against terrific odds.

268

"I, too, had fired my last cartridge. Then I saw that I was surrounded by a large number of Riffians. With a last effort I rushed at them with my bayonet, and, as a few men came to my assistance, they left me alone. We were fighting on the edge of the mountain. Not being able to see the ground I fell over the edge into the chasm. I waited there for some time, not hearing anything, not seeing any one. Then I rushed away, and while crossing the river I met the two other men. That is what I have seen."

I interrogated the other men, who told me almost the same story. This was the saddest, the most painful morning that we lived through during all the campaign. We could not even look at one another, because there was horror in the eyes of every one of us—horror at the great losses we had sustained—horror at losing our youngest and best, some of the most wonderful legionnaires that we had. Their presence was still among us. We could see their gay and bright faces! We could hear their laughter, their jokes. We could see them calm and undisturbed in battle. And we could imagine them easily in the desperate fight that they had to put up that night, surrounded on all sides by the enemy. One of the men whom I questioned uttered a phrase that revealed to me the whole situation:

"The Arabs came on us in great numbers. They

269

were like a flock of sheep in their white burnouses, so many and so thick they were."

Our men in the battalion were also under great emotion. Their faces were pale after such a night— after twice crossing the river, and standing in the cold, waiting and wanting to help those who had offered themselves as volunteers for that desperate duty. They stood around in groups. They did not talk much about the matter. There were only a few words spoken now and then. As I thought of the night's occurrences, it seemed impossible that not one of the men would return—that not one of our comrades was alive. I could not believe this awful truth.

The cavalry patrol returned. The commander came into our tent. "Dead silence all over the place," he said. "We found no one. . . ."

XI

HONOR AND FIDELITY

GARA DES MEZZIAT

June 13, 1925

TWO days after the tragic night, the battalion had its day of glory. It was cited in the orders of the army, and its flag was decorated by the Minister of War.

"The battalion of the Foreign Legion on the night of June . . . entrusted with saving by an audacious operation the remnants of the garrison in a post, who were in great extremity, has sacrified voluntarily its best elements, which disputed the honor of delivering the last defenders of the post, giving thereby an example to all of the most heroic abnegation and the most wonderful valor."

This also was a day of glory for Goulet, who had ridden across Algeria in a car bearing the words, "Here is the car of the real legionnaires, the real Gauls." Two men were to be decorated by the Minister of War with the *médaille militaire*. One of them was Goulet.

271

When Goulet was young he had been in the Colonial Army, and in 1911 he was among those battalions to deliver the city of Fez from the riotous native mob, which massacred the white population.

When this Moroccan situation developed, when he found himself once more in the atmosphere of an African campaign—so different from the Great War, in which he had also had his part—Goulet was tranformed into another man. He even looked younger. Notwithstanding the fatigue and the hardships, notwithstanding his almost twenty years of military service, notwithstanding his age and several wounds that he had received during his long service, he was one of the most cheerful men in the company.

When, on account of the heat and fatigue, the morale of the men would be low, he would cheer them up, he would find opportune words, at the most appropriate moments. He would instill new energy into them. He was a most indefatigable person. When the battalion reached a halting place and the camp was made, Goulet would offer himself for all kinds of service, which, with his experience, and with the shrewd eye of an old legionnaire, he would see were necessary.

He was the liaison man of the battalion. He would rush to the Staff to get the orders for the

272

day. He would be always the first to deliver the orders to his company.

During this period of guerrilla warfare he could be seen, his pipe in the corner of his mouth, going through fields, covering the ground under a rain of bullets. He was never touched. He was always present in the most dangerous moments, and many times he volunteered to deliver orders to one or another unit that had to be reached under almost impossible conditions. One would see him walk off on his dangerous errand, smiling, unconcerned, with a light step, shrugging his shoulders just as if he were going to join a jolly company of his comrades. He simply was unaware of danger.

Now he was to be decorated. His name was called. He stepped out of the ranks. He stood there all alone, facing the Prime Minister with hundreds of eyes upon him. The Minister pinned the decoration on the breast of Goulet and went to decorate the other man.

Goulet was there all alone, standing at attention, with his pale face and glowing eyes. Then he saw advancing toward him the tall figure of the *Maréchal*. The *Maréchal* stopped about two steps away from Goulet. He pulled off the glove from his right hand, and coming nearer to Goulet he stretched out his ungloved hand. He took the hand of Goulet, squeezed

273

it, shook it with force, and bending his head he said:

"*Mon vieux*, how many years of service have you had?"

"Nineteen years, *Monsieur le Maréchal.*"

"Nineteen years," repeated the old Chief. "That's fine. And still wanting to do it?"

"Yes, *Monsieur le Maréchal*, right to the end— to death."

"Good," said the Chief. "You will come and see me afterwards."

It was the great day of Goulet's life.

The liaison men from the General Staff came and asked Goulet to go into the tent where the generals were assembled. The *Maréchal* had him sit beside him and poured coffee into his cup. Afterwards Goulet, marching among the tents of his comrades, and receiving their congratulations, would say:

"*Médaille militaire!* Yes, the greatest honor, the greatest ambition of my life! But what is it in comparison to shaking hands with the *Maréchal?* When the *Maréchal* shook my hand he was not a chief to me, but a man. We shook hands as man to man."

And then, with his great sense of humor, he would describe how he had coffee with all these great men.

But this memorable day, when the greatest ambition of his life had been attained, when he had been

274

decorated, congratulated, and fêted, by the greatest soldier of France—it was too much for the old legionnaire. The reaction came. His nerves gave out. From that day on Goulet began to collapse. That evening, for the first time during the campaign, he got drunk, and failed to deliver orders. Everybody wanted to fête him. He became the most popular man not only among the legionnaires, but among all the troops that were near.

With his *médaille militaire* shining and glittering in the sun, wherever he went people would stop him and offer him drinks. He became a legendary person among all the troops on that front. Everyone pointed at him and said, "There is the man who was decorated by the Minister of War. There is the legionnaire who sat beside the *Maréchal.*" This popularity, this fêting, was the ruin of Goulet. He drank more and more and finally was evacuated to a hospital.

EPILOGUE

AFTER three months of campaigning, the blockade was raised from all the outposts in the region where our battalion was operating. The majority of them were blown up. A few, the largest ones and the most important strategically, were left. Their garrisons were reënforced and their armaments completed. New outposts and defenses were built on the southern bank of the Ouergha River. Whole areas of the front that could be subjected to aggression were put in a state of defense.

More battalions of the Foreign Legion arrived on the northern frontier. Once more these nomadic masons and quarrymen, builders and warriors, took up their picks and shovels. All over the country, under the torrid heat of midsummer and the rains of winter, they were toiling, sweating and singing.

Moroccan peasants under the leadership of their Caids came from the most remote districts of Morocco to join with their regular troops and with us in the pacification of the country. Confidence among the frontier tribes increased; their faces began to lose the expression of bewilderment, fear and anxiety.

The natives of the region, who had left their homes in the early spring, returned with their families and cattle and began to settle back on their land. Delegates appeared from the tribes who had gone over to join the Riffians, and reported that they were eager to get back. They feared that the Sultan of Morocco would give their land to those who had remained faithful to him, and believed in his ultimate victory

Adequate reënforcements necessary to undertake the advance into the Riff were arriving slowly during the summer of 1925. Autumn came with its heavy rains before they were finally ready to go. The roads were impassible and the active campaign had to be postponed until spring. During the winter the influence of Abd-el-Krim in the mountains was steadily diminishing. After a few engagements in the spring of 1926 he was abandoned by all the Riff tribes—even by his own. There was nothing left for him but surrender. On May 26 at Imazouene, a plateau north of Targuist, he gave himself up to the French commander.

The capitulation of the Riffian chief terminated an important epoch in the European penetration of North Africa. In Paris, on July 10, 1926, Premier Briand and General Primo de Rivera signed a new treaty which settled the questions raised by the war in the Riff. France and Spain will continue as hitherto their active coöperation in maintaining peace and establishing security in the mountains of Morocco. The tranquillity of the border zone lying between the French and Spanish protectorates was one of the most important problems discussed. Each country is to enjoy complete independence within the general scope of the treaties, which guarantee the integrity of the Sherifian empire.

Abd-el-Krim, prisoner of the French, is to be banished with his family to Reunion Island off Madagascar.

En route to Fez immediately after his capture, Abd-el-Krim passed a group of Legionnaires constructing a new road leading to the mountains. An officer of the Legion in command of the detachment wrote to me on that day as follows:

"When Abd-el-Krim passed us, the impassivity of the Moslem was for a moment broken. He stopped. He looked at our men with their picks and shovels, he saw the mass of rock being cut and the outlines of the new highway. He said: 'There is the road which brought my downfall: it followed me all the way to my stronghold.' "

After the Great War, the French High Command wondered whether the Legion would have the same spirit as before the War, because all the old legionnaires, or almost all of them, had been killed.

279

Only a few of those who went to fight in Europe remained. They, with the Germans who had remained in Morocco during the war, constituted almost the entire Legion. The High Command wondered whether the Legion would have the same fighting capacity as before the war, whether its spirit and traditions would be transmitted to the new men.

If one doubted it, a few years of life in the new Legion after the war proved doubts to be groundless. The men possessed the same spirit; and when one of the oldest officers in the Legion, one who had served in it for the past seventeen years, was asked by a French general what he thought of the *new* Legion, this old commander said:

"There is no Old Legion. There is no New Legion. There is THE French Foreign Legion."

APPENDIX

The French Foreign Legion

There have always been foreign troops in the service of
France. Charles VII had a Scottish Guard. There were
also English, Russians, Germans, Poles and Swiss that
had served under the French flag. All these were a part
of the Royal Guard. Their loyalty in 1789, as well as
in 1830, never failed. One could write a whole book
about the different foreign regiments that served under
Napoleon.

During the French Revolution, the Legislative Assembly,
after the decree of July 29, 1791, suppressed the Nassau
Regiment, No. 96, and all those who were designated as
German, Irish, Liegeians, and promulgated, the 1st of
August, 1792, a law to effect the formation of a Foreign
Legion.

This Legion was composed of infantry, cavalry and
artillery. Some days afterwards the Assembly in its fight
against all the kings, issued an appeal to the people of
Europe, and by the law of August 3, 1792, it accorded
great advantages to the noncommissioned officers and soldiers of foreign birth who would come to serve under the
banners of the Republic. This appeal was met, and by
the decree of September 4, 1792, the forming of a Foreign
Legion was prescribed.

This first Legion was called the German Legion. A
second Legion was created, which was called the Belgian
Legion. Then during the Directorate another Legion was
created which bore the name of the Italian Legion. It was
composed of four battalions of infantry, and four squads

281

of cavalry. There were also two companies of Polish Legions, one legion of the French of the north and another of the Maltese that had taken part in the expedition in Egypt. Napoleon organized half a brigade of Swiss. Then Portuguese and Spanish regiments.

Under the Restoration, by order of the King, on September 16, 1814, the Colonial Foreign Regiment was organized. By the Royal Order of September 16, 1815, all the regiments of foreign infantry were reorganized in one royal foreign legion, which afterwards took the name of Hohenlohe. The two Royal Orders of July 18, 1816 formed four regiments of Swiss Guards. Finally, on February 22, 1821, the Hohenlohe Legion was reorganized in one regiment composed of three battalions, which took the name of Hohenlohe Regiment.

In 1830 the Swiss regiments were disbanded, and the Hohenlohe Regiment was dissolved also on January 5, 1831. But on the 9th of March in that year the first foreign Legion was organized. And it was only then that the existence of the Foreign Legion as we know it, began.

This new corps could be employed only outside of the continental territory of the Kingdom. Enlistments were for three years at least. The maximum was five years, with the privilege of reënlisting for two to five years more. A recruit had to be at least eighteen years old, and not more than forty. This Legion was made up of companies in which the men were of the same nationality and spoke the same language. But race hatred was alive even then. There were sharp conflicts and collisions between these companies. So in 1835 the men of different nationalities were mixed together, and since then this system, which proved excellent, has been used.

In August, 1831, the battalion went to Algeria and served there with distinction. On June 24, 1832, Colonel Combes, its new chief, landed in Algeria with the flag of the Legion, given to it by the King. In all the battles against Abd-el-Kader at Sidi-Chabal, at the battle of Arzew, Mostaganem and of Muley-Ismael, June 26, 1835, one finds the Legion courageously doing its duty.

On January 28, 1835, by a treaty between France, England, Spain and Portugal, it was ageed that the Foreign Legion should pass into the service of Spain to help Isabelle II, the daughter of Ferdinand VII and Marie Christine-Bourbon. Among the feats of arms in Spain one counts the resistance of the blockhousᴄ of Tera-pegui, April 26, 1836, where 6,000 Carlists fought for six hours against 1,000 legionnaires and could not take them. At Huesca, March 24, 1837, out of 4,000 men of the Legion, there were 350 wounded and killed, among whom were twenty officers.

Finally, on January 17, 1839, the Legion was disbanded. Never before had it had such a hard campaign. The Carlists shot the wounded and the prisoners. The Spanish government paid the legionnaires very poorly, and the Legion was recalled from Spain.

On December 16, 1835, Louise-Philippe ordered the formation of a new Legion, which in the beginning went to Spain to help the old Legion; and at the end of 1836 it went to Algeria. At that time the majority of the new recruits were Dutch.

All during the years of fighting in Algeria, the Legion distinguished itself and proved its great valor. There is not a mountain, a ravine, a valley or a native town in the mountains or in the desert, where the bodies of these legionnaires do not lie. From east to west they went, and everywhere they were the same—they were men of iron. They were never bent by the extreme tension of battle, and when there was no war they built houses and cities—they cleared up wild steppes. The city of Bél-Abbés was built entirely by the Legion. The richly cultivated plains around it were due to the legionnaires. One cannot enumerate all the battles, all the campaigns of the Legion. One cannot name all the places where they fought. The Legion was one of the greatest factors in the conquest of Algeria for France, and the officers were always most proud to command these soldiers.

From the beginning of the war in the East, the first and second regiments of the Foreign Legion were designated to take part in the army and to fight against Russia. In June and July of 1854, they landed at Gallipoli, and were a part of the 5th Division of the Oriental Army.

During the epidemic of cholera, when men were dying by thousands, the legionnaires suffered less than the others because of their campaign habits. In the first days of September the Legion left Turkey to go to the Crimea, and they landed in Eupatoria. General Canrobert and Maréchal de Saint-Arnaud, former officers of the Legion, directed the armies. At Alma, September 20th, the legionnaires were represented by their best companies, forming one battalion which, according to General Canrobert, had to be the chief factors of the struggle and made the first onslaught against the Russian troops. The hard and terrible days of the siege of Sebastopol began—the hard life in the trenches. In cold, and rain, and snow, nothing could daunt the courage of the legionnaires, who had a most active part in the many attacks and counter-attacks against the Russians. They were noted for their impetuosity while charging with bayonets.

"The war in the Crimea," writes Colonel Villebous-Mareuil, "could not but show vividly the great military valor of the troops in the Foreign Legion. In this terrible campaign, where the endurance, the various aptitudes, the innate bravery of our army are prodigious, the legionnaires have forged for themselves an outstanding reputation."

Different regiments of the Legion went to Italy in March and April, 1859, to take part in the brilliant battle of Magenta. They inflicted great losses on the Austrians and set an example to the other troops all during this campaign. There was never any confusion in their ranks and the battalions went into battle just as orderly as they would have gone on parade.

On June 12, 1864, when Emperor Maximilian and his wife, Empress Charlotte, made their entry into Mexico, they had with them a Legion composed of 6,000 Austrian volunteers and 1,500 Belgian. Originally the legionnaires had not been chosen to go on this expedition, but when the officers of the Legion learned that only the Zouaves were going, they protested and addressed a petition directly to the Emperor asking him to permit them to go to Mexico. In the files of the French Foreign Legion one can find many battles recorded which took place during this fierce Mexican campaign.

In 1867 the Foreign Legion went back to Algeria.

In 1870, during the war with Germany, the battalions of the Foreign Legion in Algeria took the place of the French troops who were there and were being sent back to France. Among the legionnaires at that time was a soldier who afterwards became a king—Peter of Serbia.

On October 8, 1870, the Foreign Legion having left the depot in Algeria, all the soldiers of German nationality left Oran for France. The Legion was then increased by many volunteers, who joined it to fight against the Germans. On the 29th of March the Foreign Legion was sent to Paris to fight against the Commune.

Those of the Legion who remained in Algeria during the War of 1870 had a great task to perform, because of the many rebels among the natives. The years that followed the war with Germany in the 70's were calm in Algeria, and the legionnaires were occupied in the work of constructing roads and towns. Immediately after this war the majority of the recruits in the Legion were Alsatians and Lorrainians, who, not wanting to serve in the German army, deserted and went into the Foreign

285

Legion in order to become French citizens after their years of service were completed.

The Legion fought in China also. In 1883 the Legion left Algeria for Hai-Phong and Hanoi.

The Legion distinguished itself in succeeding years in all the battles that were fought in Indo-China and Tonkin.

In 1892 the Legion participated in the expedition into Dahomey.

The first detachment of the Legion came to Morocco, landing at Casablanca in 1907. They took part in the pacification of the Chaouia. Since then the Legion has taken part in all the work of pacification that has been undertaken by France in this part of Northern Africa.

During the Great War in 1914-1918, the ranks of the Legion were increased by hundreds and thousands of volunteers that joined the French colors. The Legion distinguished itself in all the battles in which it took part from the beginning of the War until the end. The Legion flag was decorated many times. In August, 1914, as soon as hostilities with Germany started, an immense throng of foreigners stormed all the recruiting bureaus and asked to be admitted to service in the French Army. The sentiment that guided them was simple and honorable—they were confident in the justice of the French cause, and they wanted to take part in the tragic events that followed the declaration of War. The government then decided to create marching battalions of the Legion which would be made up of these young volunteers mixed in among the older legionnaires.

All these new recruits were engaged, not for five years, but for the duration of the War. Instruction of the volunteers began without delay in many of the cities of France. Among these battalions was an Italian battalion commanded by the grandson of Garibaldi. Fifty-one nations were represented in this new battalion. The Swiss formed the majority of the foreign volunteers; after them came the Spanish; then the Luxemburgians; and then all the old legionnaires of Belgian nationality asked permission from their government to join the French Foreign Legion. There were Dutch, Turks, Egyptians, Persians, and also many Americans.

All through the Great War the Foreign Legion distinguished itself in many of the great battles, winning many decorations.

(1)

THE END